H.I.T.
Investing

H.I.T.
Investing

Strong Returns Through High-Impact Investing Leveraging Technology

MAHESH JOSHI

PENGUIN
BUSINESS

An imprint of Penguin Random House

PENGUIN BUSINESS

Penguin Business is an imprint of the Penguin Random House group of companies
whose addresses can be found at global.penguinrandomhouse.com

Published by Penguin Random House India Pvt. Ltd
4th Floor, Capital Tower 1, MG Road,
Gurugram 122 002, Haryana, India

First published in Penguin Business by Penguin Random House India 2025

ISBN 9780143472056

Typeset in Adobe Caslon Pro by MAP Systems, Bengaluru, India
Printed at Thomson Press India Ltd, New Delhi

www.penguin.co.in

Contents

Preface

Money is one of mankind's most paradoxical inventions. Its invention allowed our ancestors to break out of the constraints of the barter system, where they had to physically exchange goods and services. As societies grew and migration and trade connected the seas, bartering likely became increasingly difficult and complex. If you didn't have the necessary goods for a direct trade, you might spend days or even weeks trying to find a suitable solution to break the logjam. Money allowed society to function more easily on a wider scale. Almost everything in this world—except maybe the priceless moments that MasterCard tells you about—can be quantified with this one variable. Its simplicity allowed everyone to pursue accumulating money as a goal. However, money is still complex enough to cause disagreements among the smartest financial brains in treasury departments across the world, and global economy crashes or surges that can and do reverberate across the world.

Having spent nearly two decades in the investment field, I've dedicated a significant amount of time thinking about money. As a private equity investor, I invest in companies most of the time that are not listed on the stock market, with the hope that we will generate good returns on our investment. For that to happen, the companies that we invest in have to efficiently utilize the capital we provide, in order to offer a product or service that is useful to its customers. In return, those customers must be willing to part with their hard-earned money, to help companies make good profits and, in turn, help investors make good returns.

For a long period of time, companies across the world have worked on achieving high returns by simply pricing products right, to create aspirations in the minds of consumers and, in turn, make better profits. Businesses sometimes price their products higher just because they want to create the perception that what they are offering is at an absolute premium. Take a look at the consumer map and you will see what I mean: premium products and services. The world is full of such businesses—from Moët Hennessy Louis Vuitton SE (LVMH) to Apple. Companies like these do not price products to make them available at the lowest cost. By doing this, they often miss out on serving a larger market. These companies have been able to sustain this pricing by creating moats, often in distribution in addition to recognizable brands, that prevent other players from disrupting them.

I first noticed this when I started my career in equity research in India in 2005. My key responsibility then was to make recommendations, which were backed by solid research, on buying and selling the right stocks to institutional investors, i.e. mutual funds and foreign institutional investors (FIIs) investing in India. One of the sectors I spent a lot of time on was fast moving consumer goods (FMCG). I used to cover stocks such as Hindustan Unilever, ITC, Colgate and Dabur. These companies were unique. Most of them consistently delivered return on equity north of 30 per cent (and often more than 50 per cent) with little to no debt, and, more importantly, did not require much capital expenditure or working capital to grow. In fact, some companies, such as Hindustan Unilever, were famous for operating on negative working capital by essentially taking cash immediately from their distributors while getting credit from their suppliers and paying them later. This means that the more they grew, the more cash they generated, not just from the resultant profits but also from the negative working capital cycle. As a result, these companies were essentially considered cash-generating machines.

Now, companies like the ones I've mentioned above did not sell any innovative products. They were selling everyday products such as soaps, shampoos and toothpastes. While those products were marketed as new and innovative, in most cases, there was nothing new about them, and practically, you and I could manufacture those products with a little bit of effort. Why, then, were they able to generate such high profits and maintain such strong control over the supply chain that they could squeeze it? This was a question I grappled with a lot. After spending lot of time analysing these companies, I reached the conclusion, which was not very different from many people in the industry, that there were two areas that these companies had mastered—building a strong brand in the minds of the consumers and ensuring easy availability of products with a distribution network that reached most corners across the country.

There have been very few cases of new brands making a significant dent in the market in India across categories. Over time, I developed the belief that pricing products and services at a premium by building a brand was necessary not just to drive profits but also the sustainability of the business. Unless consumers think that you are offering a differentiated product or service and are willing to pay a premium for that product or service, it could be easy for other companies to disrupt your business. The more I analysed business patterns, the more convinced of this belief did I become. I felt that this was the only way to build a business. I carried this belief with me when I became an investor in 2007. The same belief was reinforced over the next decade as I interacted with top managements and CXOs across various sectors as an investor.

Little did I know, that one of the pillars of this thesis—control over distribution—was already on shaky ground. In 2002, Jeff Bezos, the founder of Amazon, observed, 'Your margin is my opportunity.' It was a telling remark, because since then, we've seen the kind of disruption that Amazon has caused across sectors. In 2023, retail e-commerce sales accounted for over 19 per cent of overall retail sales worldwide, and Statista predicts that, by 2027, e-commerce will make up nearly a quarter of total global retail sales.[1]

E-commerce has allowed companies to bypass regular distribution channels and reach the customer directly. In India alone, the e-commerce industry is estimated to grow from USD 70 billion at present to USD 325 billion by 2030, according to the Invest India report.[2] The share of e-commerce in overall retail in India is around 7.8 per cent. The buyers on e-commerce platforms are also expected to touch 500 million by 2030. The sector is growing at 27 per cent a year, which means it will double every three years. As a result, we have seen a plethora of brands, competing with the biggies with at least a fair chance of success, if not entirely at par.

Technology has not only neutralized the distribution strength of established businesses but also expanded reach to previously inaccessible regions and customers, creating an environment for new entrants to disrupt the status quo. This is a welcome change when we are trying to address multiple challenges such as climate change and food security. Indeed, there are many outstanding businesses that are now focused on addressing these challenges. This has resulted in significant opportunities for investors to support the scaling of these businesses.

In 2017, after having spent a decade in private equity in India, I joined an impact investment firm which focused on improving the affordability and accessibility of healthcare, financial products and services for low- and middle-income people across emerging markets. Truth be told, I joined the firm because I found the opportunity to cover wider geography, including South Asia and South-east Asia, to be an interesting challenge after having spent my entire career focused on India. When I first joined the firm, it seemed like a constraint to find businesses which were driving affordability by offering quality products and services at reasonable value without charging the customers the premium for the perception of their brand. In hindsight, my own beliefs that were built up over a decade were constraining me. However, once I set my mind to finding such businesses, I discovered remarkable ones that were clearly poised to be long-term winners, especially since it's even tougher for competitors when someone is already delivering great value to their customers.

I also did some research on how other impact investors, who invested with the same objective of addressing the essential needs of low- and middle-income consumers, were performing. The results were very promising. However, like my old self, there were many who questioned the value in this investing approach, which is regularly adopted by the impact investors. In 2022, I was a panellist at an investor event. We were speaking about impact investing. At the end of the panel discussion, we were asked a very interesting question by a member of the audience: 'Why do impact investors label themselves as such, if they can generate commercial returns?' This question made me think about the best approach with which we can address such scepticism.

A light bulb went off in my head when I was watching *The Game Changers*, a Netflix documentary which challenged the prevalent notion that you can be strong only when you eat meat. It introduces us to athletes from various sports—ranging from long-distance running and cycling to powerlifting and Ultimate Fighting Championship (UFC)—who were excelling at the top of their field while being vegans. In fact, they attributed their success to their vegan lifestyle. This documentary busts all the long-standing myths about animal protein and shows how being a vegan helps deliver better performance and is fundamentally a better approach to being at the top of your game. I noticed a parallel between the impact investing myths I was trying to bust and the myths on veganism that the documentary busted. The documentary demonstrates the advantages of being vegan by highlighting the benefits experienced by top athletes who embraced this lifestyle, while also backing it up with research explaining why it was effective. I felt a similar approach could work for impact investing.

For those new to the world of impact investing, it can be simply defined as identifying a cause that is important to you and investing with the objective to support that cause. We will define 'what is impact investing?' in Chapter 5. We will also demonstrate how it is done by sharing examples of outstanding businesses that the leading impact investors have invested in and how these businesses are making the world a better place. I have written this book in the hope of making the world of impact investing more accessible—for the man in the audience who asked the question that made me truly reflect on what I do and why I do it. For this reason, I have kept the tone easy and conversational. I use the word 'conversational' quite literally. It is based on my own conversations with eight impact investors, who invest in equity in private markets and are usually labelled as venture capital investors, if they invest in start-ups and early-stage businesses and private equity investors, if they invest in mature or growth stage businesses.

Just as the documentary showcased athletes from different disciplines to prove that veganism works universally, I chose investors who operate across various stages and geographies to demonstrate that this approach is effective everywhere—

from early seed-stage ventures and growth-stage companies to traditional profitable enterprises and projects. The investors covered in this book have chosen to take the responsibility of building a better world for future generations, and while doing that, they are generating impressive returns. In that sense, they are challenging a lot of assumptions, but as you will see, their strategy is grounded in first principles. These investors are truly making a difference to the world we live in by investing mostly in companies that leverage technology to deliver not only high impact but also strong returns. We call this approach H.I.T. (High Impact through Technology) investing. The word technology does not refer to just information technology but also includes innovations and new approaches across sectors, including energy, climate and finance.

Introduction

'We do not inherit the earth from our ancestors.
We borrow it from our children'
—Wendell Berry

We are at an interesting juncture in the history of mankind. On the one hand, there are serious questions about the sustainability of the world. In 2024, we used up earth's resources by 1 August, which means we are spending a third of the year borrowing from our future generations.[1] In other words, we need more than 1.5 Planet Earths to sustain our needs each year. Over the last half a century, we have been consistently doing this. It does not take too much wisdom to conclude that this is not sustainable in the long run. The world is significantly behind schedule in achieving the Sustainable Development Goals (SDGs) set by the United Nations in 2015, according to a new UN report. These goals, which encompass a wide range of areas, including poverty reduction, hunger eradication and environmental protection, were intended to be achieved by 2030. Released just before the UN Summit of the Future in September 2024, the report cautioned that a 'business as usual' approach will not suffice and called for a major overhaul.

On the other hand, innovation is progressing on a massive scale and gives us the optimism that solutions to most of the challenges are within our grasp.

The sustainability of this world is one of the fundamental tenets of investing. Almost all investing is based on arriving at present value by discounting cash flows from far into the future. Investing not based on discounting of cash flow is usually labelled as speculation. While every investor assumes sustainability while valuing assets, there are a few working towards making it true. After all, there has to be significant value waiting to be unlocked from improving the probability of future cash flows of all the businesses in the world. This book will uncover the secrets and strategies of some of these investors across the globe who are addressing critical challenges and are delivering excellent returns while doing so.

When you talk about anybody who is doing well in any field, the first questions that come to our mind are:

- How are they doing it?
- What are the techniques that they use?
- What is the secret sauce behind their success?

This book will address questions like these. However, before we get to those questions, we will discuss an even more important concept. As consultants like to say, 'where to play' is more important than 'how to play'. It is a concept that is very easy to absorb for most people. For instance, most of the companies in a sector do very well when that particular sector is booming and often times is an important determinant in success. It applies even to individuals and hence choosing which sector to be part of is an important decision from a career perspective. Like with most things in life, 'where to play?' is much clearer in hindsight.

The athletes in *The Game Changers* documentary chose to follow a vegan diet only because they thought it would make them better athletes and increase their probability of winning. In the same way, the investors pursuing impact investing with the intent to generate commercial returns are doing it because of the opportunity to unlock returns. The first part of this book will shed light on the opportunities in addressing critical challenges and explain why the investors featured here are benefiting from the path they have chosen to follow. The second part of the book addresses how each investor is going about it, with a dedicated chapter for each of the eight investors. Each chapter details the journey of the investor and the motivation behind choosing to address the global challenges, their investment strategy and performance with case studies on businesses that help drive their performance.

In each chapter on the investors, we will dive deep into how they are managing the four critical aspects of the private investing process:

a) **Origination**: Finding the opportunities to invest. Unlike in public markets, where all companies are accessible to everyone, the private market opportunities are not always accessible to everyone and hence ensuring that access is very important.

b) **Assessment of investments**: Evaluating the investments. Again, unlike in public markets, where data is widely available and can be relied upon, a significant amount of due diligence is required in private markets.

c) **Portfolio Management**: Private investors have the opportunity to play an active role in helping their investee companies grow and achieve their objectives. We will cover the levers used by investors to add value to their portfolio companies.

d) **Exit**: While most public market investors ensure exit by participating in liquid stocks, private investors must work hard to create liquidity events such as IPO and sale of shares. In fact, a running joke in private markets is that 'you know you are with a private equity or venture capital investor if he looks for an exit sign even before entering'. We will highlight how these investors are positioning themselves for attractive returns.

As we dive into the investment strategies of investors, you'll notice that we explore each of the above topics for nearly all of them. Additionally, most of the investor chapters also touch on two other topics—portfolio construction and approaches to impact assessment and measurement.

To ensure that we can cover a wide spectrum of strategies, we have chosen private equity and venture capital investors across geographies and across sectors. A brief overview of those investors is below:

Investor	Geography	Sector
AC Ventures	Indonesia	Technology (diversified)
Apis Partners	Global	Financial Services
Capria Ventures	Global emerging markets	Technology (other than fintech)
Future Planet Capital	UK and Developed markets	Diversified
Lok Capital	India	Financial Inclusion
Quona	Global emerging markets	Fintech
SDCL	Europe and the US	Energy efficiency
Verdane	Europe	Technology (including Decarbonization)

The investors are also well diversified across the stages they invest in. Capria and Future Planet focus on very early-stage ventures and provide seed capital, while Quona and AC Ventures support slightly evolved ventures that have developed a market and have started generating revenues. Apis and Lok Capital mostly invest in profitable enterprises or those with a clear path to profitability and provide growth capital. SDCL invests in projects driving energy efficiency in addition to providing growth capital.

If you prefer case studies to theory, feel free to jump straight into Part 2. Within Part 2, each of the investor chapters is separate and you can choose to read them in any order you prefer. We have arranged them in alphabetical order of their names. In Part 1 though, I would suggest reading the chapters in order.

Part 1

The Playground for H.I.T. Investing

1

The Microfinance Revolution

'Nothing is more powerful than an idea
whose time has come'
—Victor Hugo

Microfinance has been one of the biggest areas of focus for several impact investors globally. The small loans provided by microfinance institutions have provided springboards for millions of people to jump out of poverty. The seeds for microfinance to become such a powerful tool for change were sown way back in the '80s by a young man from Bangladesh, Mohammad Yunus, who was awarded Nobel Peace Prize in 2006 for his efforts.

When Bangladesh won independence from Pakistan in 1971, Mohammad Yunus was away in the United States. He was teaching at Middle Tennessee State University, Tennessee but he had always kept an eye on the events of his country. Now that Bangladesh stood free and independent, Yunus knew it was time to return home. He wanted to contribute to economic development, and with his degrees and qualifications, he knew that he had the skills to do so. In 1974, Yunus returned to Bangladesh, taking a teaching position as the head of the Economics Department at Chittagong University. In the

meantime, he took a good look around him. Bangladesh—
or East Pakistan as it used to be known—had always been a
poor region. However, these early years of independence only
deepened the grinding poverty, exacerbated by a devastating
famine in 1974 that began in the district of Rangpur and
then spread across the rest of the country. Matters were made
worse by the wider geopolitics of the region, when the Nixon
administration suddenly cut off food aid to Bangladesh on the
grounds that it was earning money by exporting jute bags to
Cuba. With an annual per capita income of USD 133.60 at the
time of its liberation, Bangladesh was in crisis.[1]

Yunus was rapidly getting disillusioned with academia and
its inability to make change possible on the ground. He was
despondent and used to wander through the mud-clogged lanes
of villages near Chittagong University, and during one of those
visits to a nearby village, he happened to see a woman weaving
elegant bamboo stools outside her decrepit shack. He was
deeply struck by her skill, especially in contrast to the poverty
of her surroundings. After a little persuasion, the woman told
Yunus that the materials she needed cost the equivalent of five
US dollars, which she had secured from a loan shark. But the
terms of the loan were so harsh that she was unable to make a
living for herself on the open market. Instead, she was forced to
sell her entire inventory back to the lender, at whatever price he
dictated. In a *Time* magazine interview, Yunus recalled likening
what he had heard to slavery: 'For the sake of five dollars
someone with such beautiful skills can be turned into a slave.'[2]

Yunus then did something simple that changed the course
of his life—and, in a broader sense, the way finance and
commerce were conducted worldwide. He lent the woman the
five dollars she needed under the loose understanding that she
should repay him whenever she could. He also encouraged her
to tell other villagers in a similar predicament to come to him.

Word spread, and eventually forty-two women came forward, to whom Yunus lent a total of USD 27.

This experience made him realize the immense potential in offering credit at reasonable interest rates to poor and vulnerable people. Since banks would not lend to such people, considering their high-risk profiles, Yunus decided to borrow himself to lend it forward to these poor people. He reached out to many institutions and finally secured a credit line from Janata Bank in December 1976 and started lending to the poor people in Jobra. Out of that simple act was spawned a 'microcredit' research project whose success became the Grameen (Village) Bank in October 1983.

In time, the Grameen Bank would go on to become far more than a bank. It would become a phenomenon, mushrooming to over a hundred developing countries across the globe. Even in the United States, Grameen Bank is present across thirty-five American cities, lending over USD 4 billion to predominantly minority women. It managed USD 1 billion in loan disbursement in 2023, with repayment rates consistently above 99 per cent. Overall, more than 94 per cent of Grameen loans worldwide have gone to women, who suffer disproportionately from poverty and are more likely to use earnings to help their families than men.[3] This kind of performance is difficult to find even in banks of high pedigree serving top notch customers with great profiles. In fact, it is a gold standard when you consider that these loans were completely unsecured without any collateral.

So, what is the secret sauce that has driven this performance? One of the critical changes to the lending model implemented by the Grameen Bank was to group their customers into associations. This method had several advantages. Since loan amounts were small, clubbing them together made the disbursement and collection process easier. Correspondingly, it reduced the burden of operating costs and helped organize the necessary training for these groups in order to build their businesses. However, the key innovation of Grameen Bank's method was to make the said group responsible for the credit received by the whole group, rather than just the individual's own credit. This led to very low default rates. The borrowers benefited from extremely reasonable interest rates and there was no need to offer any collateral.

In essence, what Muhammad Yunus and Grameen Bank were able to achieve through this model was to convert a high-risk customer into a credit worthy one. In economic terms, this invention can be described by the two-by-two matrix below.

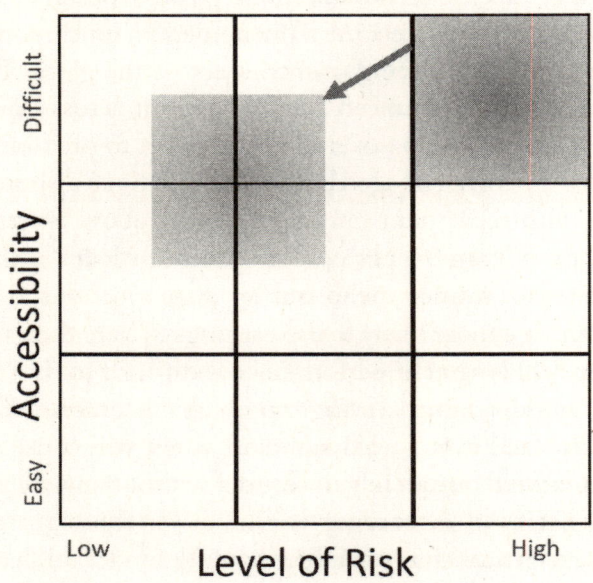

Figure 1: Microfinance has changed the risk and accessibility profile of the borrower

Essentially, what the above figure shows is that before the Grameen Bank transformed the world of microfinance, any lender, including banks, usually determined the interest cost based on the risk associated with the borrower, as well as the cost of reaching that customer. The cost as a percentage of the loan increases as the loan gets smaller, leaving poor people who needed small amounts of money with no option but to turn to loan sharks. Given that these were customers who could not offer the lender any collateral or even furnish documents supporting their existing sources of income, it was hard to underwrite such loans.

The Grameen Bank changed this game by taking an inaccessible customer and improving their accessibility by clubbing them into groups based on proximity and familiarity. It also reduced the risk by leveraging social bonds in the absence of collateral and was able to offer loans at lower interest rates to customers on account of lower risk. This process was termed microfinance or microcredit.

Microfinance Experiments Begin in India in 1980s

Given the model's global success, it's not difficult to imagine that it would find a good home in India as well. But what is usually overlooked is the fact that India had seen its own attempts at microfinance, long before Muhammad Yunus's Grameen Bank took the world by storm. In the 1970s, banks' share in rural credit rose from 3 per cent to 15 per cent, which created growth of non-agricultural output in rural areas and an expansion of small business activity.[4] According to Philip Mader, this spurt led to a collapse in the informal credit extended by moneylenders, traders and landlords, whose shares in household debt fell by more than half in the 1970s, while the share of household debt to formal institutions doubled.[5] A large portion of lending to poor people in India in the 1970s and 1980s also came from the state through the Integrated Rural Development Program

(IRDP), whose subsidized credit for farming improvements and livelihood diversification projects was not considered an operational success, though it led to 22 per cent decline in the level of poverty amongst IRDP families and 7 per cent of families crossing the poverty line. The key learning was that the IRDP families also needed support in areas such as marketing in addition to credit facilities.[6] However, initiatives such as IRDP brought many poorer households in India in contact with formal sector debt. Then, of course, there was the movement for women's economic empowerment, led by the 'gentle revolutionary' Ela Bhatt—fondly known as Elaben. In 1972, Elaben founded the Self-Employed Women's Association (SEWA), a trade union that has around two million members. She set up the SEWA Cooperative Bank in 1974. Today, SEWA is one of the largest cooperatives working for women, with a base of over two million members from around eighteen states in the country and in neighbouring nations.[7] Under Elaben's able and unique leadership, the SEWA cooperative movement of informal women workers grew to be the largest of its kind in the world. She led from the front, forging new paths towards an equitable and inclusive world that she deeply believed in, and one that was respectful of the planet. She is one of the greatest examples of Indian attempts at microfinance in the 1980s and 1990s.

Based on this experience, microfinance began in India with state-sponsored Self-Help Group (SHG) lending models from the late 1980s. These SHGs started in 1984, when the cooperatives managed by Myrada, a parastatal agency working particularly in the South of India, collapsed and many members began organizing their own groups for savings accumulation. Myrada and the National Bank for Agriculture and Rural Development (NABARD) together trained and expanded these groups, linking them to banks. In 1996, this linkage was mainstreamed by the

Reserve Bank of India (RBI) and had garnered the support of the World Bank by the dawn of the new millennium.[8]

The liberalization of India's economy and its financial sector after 1991 changed the composition of lending once again, with credit from the private sector rising and with the ascendancy of MFIs and SHGs, even as the state remained a driving force in the background.[9]

Microfinance Takes Off in India in the Twenty-First Century

In the twenty-first century, India finally saw its real expansion in the microfinance sector, with several impact investors, including the ones covered in this book such as Lok Capital, focusing on microfinance in the country, in the early 2000s. Development Financial Institutions[10] (DFIs) such as International Finance Corporation (IFC) and British International Investment (BII) also started supporting this space with capital. Aided by their support, the sector grew to Rs 17,264 crores (USD 3 billion) by 2012. In July 2012, Reserve Bank of India created a new category of Non-Banking Financial Companies (NBFCs) specifically for microfinance institutions.[11] With strong regulatory oversight, the microfinance sector has grown more than twenty times, since 2012, to reach Rs 4,33,697[12] crores (USD 52 billion) at a CAGR of 30.8 per cent in 2024.

The growth experienced by the microfinance companies in India led to early entrants evolving into Small Finance Banks (SFBs), a new banking license introduced by the Reserve Bank of India with a focus on driving inclusion, by primarily extending basic banking services to unserved and underserved sections, including small and marginal farmers, small business units, micro and small industries and unorganized entities. SFBs also function as savings vehicles, providing credit facilities to small business units, micro and small industries, small and marginal farmers, and other unorganized sectors through advanced technology and low-cost operations. The early SFB licenses were given largely to the established microfinance lenders in the country, including Bandhan, Equitas, Jana, Ujjivan and Utkarsh.

There are not many sectors that can deliver a 30 per cent CAGR growth over nearly two decades. This growth has been driven by the substantial capital attracted to the space, owing to these companies' ability to generate strong returns over the long term, supported by low default rates in the sector. This sector has proven to be resilient across several disruptions to micro enterprises that India faced over the last decade including, demonetization in 2017, GST implementation in 2018 and COVID-19 pandemic during 2020–21.

Above all, the growth has been driven by the significant value created by unlocking the productivity of people at the bottom of the pyramid. The microfinance sector has helped fuel the dreams of those people by helping them become their own agents of change. It has provided springboards to lift millions of people out of poverty. This does not just benefit those people, but the entire nation because these people now have the purchasing power to drive the demand for products and services, thereby fueling GDP growth.

Investors who backed this sector have made substantial returns. A good example is Lok Capital (covered in this book), which focused largely on the microfinance sector. Lok Capital's Fund I generated top quartile returns while Fund II was in the top decile for their respective vintages.[13] Microfinance in India is a good example of what we can achieve when we invest with the objective of creating real value, which is what impact investing attempts to do. And yes, as with any investment, when executed well, the returns are likely to follow.

2

Trillions Are Needed

'Predicting rain doesn't count. Building arks does'
—Warren Buffett

One of the questions I get asked often when I talk about the success of microfinance is why investors were so successful in this area. I understand where this question comes from. However, before we answer it, it's worth stepping back to agree on what money really is—especially since, as investors, we're trying to generate more of it.

Money is one of the most interesting and probably the most productive inventions of mankind. As human beings, we pay for products and services using money and equate money to the cost of those products and services. While it is the case, no product or service itself asks for money. It is the producer or provider or that product or service that asks for money. In that sense, money is a way of quantifying human effort.

Money Is Human Effort Quantified

Money has helped us move away from the barter system of the old, which was essentially trading human effort on

different products and services. As a medium of exchange,
money has helped us quantify that human effort over the
ages. At this point, you're right to think that you don't always
pay only for human effort. After all, the Louis Vuittons and
Guccis of the world do not require as much effort, right?
That's true, but only to an extent. As a customer, you're still
paying the company for what it can command for its effort.
Now, how *much* are you able to command for your effort might
vary depending on several aspects, the key being scarcity,
and in the case of luxury brands, the impression of scarcity
created by them.

Money enables collaboration of human effort to create
value. Milton Friedman[1] explains this collaboration by taking
the manufacturing of a pencil as an example.[2] A pencil
comes into existence through the collaboration of many
people working together. The pencil manufacturer sources
the wood from a woodcutter who uses a saw produced by
another individual or firm. The saw, in turn, is made from steel
supplied by a steel manufacturer, who relies on iron ore mined
by yet another firm. Other components of the pencil, such as
graphite and rubber, are similarly sourced from different firms.
So, if you look at it like that, no single individual manufactures
a single pencil. In effect, it is the effort of thousands of people
who probably don't speak the same language, practice different
religions, but came together to make a product. In Friedman's
words, 'When you go down to the store and buy this pencil,
you are, in effect, trading a few minutes of your time for a few
seconds of the time of all of those thousands of people. What
brought them together and induced them to cooperate to
make this pencil? There was no commissar sending out offices,
sending out orders from some central office. It was the magic
of the price system, the impersonal operation of prices that

brought them together, and got them to cooperate to make this pencil so that you could have it for a trifling sum.'[3]

The most important point for the purpose of our discussion is that money allows you to exchange a fraction of *your* effort for a fraction of the effort of *other* people. When you have money, you have the ability to call upon people's effort to get the product or service you want. It is one of the reasons why power is equated to wealth. When you are in a powerful position, you have the ability to guide human effort in the direction you desire. However, this is a digression from the point at hand.

If money is human effort quantified and you want to generate more of it, it is not hard to conclude that unlocking human productivity will go a long way in achieving those outcomes. However, there are other factors that you need to get right. But once you have invested in something that creates value in the system, you are in a very good position to capture a part of that value. It is the reason why financial inclusion in general and microfinance in particular has been one of the biggest drivers of returns for investors. It unlocks human effort that was otherwise idle because of a lack of access to financial services. However, microfinance is not the only area where such leaps are possible. There are many other areas including education and health, which can help us create significant value. The sector that deserves extra attention is one of the biggest challenges of our time—climate.

Climate is a unique challenge. If we do not address it, it can lead to severe destruction. Climate change can potentially lead to loss of lives on a mass scale. In more quantifiable terms, a climate crisis can obliterate a significant amount of what we call wealth, which is essentially the ability to call on future human effort. However, one of the biggest conundrums of our time is that nations are not willing to prioritize these goals.

Why? Because they worry about the impact on their economy. It's a vicious cycle. Essentially, nations are competing with each other for the ability to call upon more human effort in future, at the cost of massive destruction of overall human effort.

I do not intend to trivialize this issue. Many developing countries are reluctant to shoulder the burden of a problem that, to a large extent, they rightly believe was created by wealthy nations.

In his book, *How to Avoid a Climate Disaster*, Microsoft founder and philanthropist Bill Gates writes, 'Unless we move fast toward zero, bad things (and probably many of them) will happen well within most people's lifetime, and very bad things will happen within a generation. Even if climate change doesn't rank as an existential threat to humanity, it will make most people worse off, and it will make the poorest even poorer. It will keep getting worse until we stop adding greenhouse gases to the atmosphere, and it deserves to be as much of a priority as health and education.'[4] He also points to several solutions that are already operating offer a Green Discount, which means people save by adopting a green solution, compared to its fossil fuel alternative. It is these solutions that we need to accelerate while we make significant efforts to create breakthrough solutions, in order to solve these problems at scale.

Now, I don't mean to say that no effort is being made at all in order to achieve these objectives. My point is that the scale of the effort required far exceeds the effort that is being put in. In 2015, the United Nations launched Sustainable Development Goals (SDGs), with the objective to mobilize resources towards some of these large challenges. The seventeen SDGs are:

Figure 2: United Nations sustainable development goals

Source: United Nations Sustainable Development, 'Communications Material', https://www.un.org/sustainabledevelopment/news/ communications-material/

These seventeen SDGs can be broadly classified into four key buckets:

- <u>Planet:</u> SDGs that target addressing climate challenges and building sustainable ecosystems. These include Clean Water and Sanitation (SDG 6), Affordable and Clean Energy (SDG 7), Sustainable Cities and Communities (SDG 11), Responsible Consumption and Production (SDG 12), Climate Action (SDG 13), Life Below Water (SDG 14) and Life on Land (SDG 15).
- <u>People:</u> SDGs that target improvement in people's lives. These include No Poverty (SDG 1), Zero Hunger (SDG 2), Good Health and Well Being (SDG 3) and Quality Education (SDG 4).

- <u>Equality</u>: SDGs that are intended to drive inclusion and equality. These include Gender Equality (SDG 5), Reduced Inequalities (SDG 10) and Peace, Justice and Strong Institutions (SDG 16).
- <u>Development</u>: SDGs that focus on leveraging industry and private enterprises for the achievement of targets. These include Decent Work and Economic Growth (SDG 8), Industry, Innovation and Infrastructure (SDG 9) and Partnerships for the Goals (SDG 17).

Now, in 2024, the United Nations estimates that USD 5–7 trillion per annum[5] is required by developing countries alone, just to achieve the goals set under SDGs.

3

And Trillions Can Be Made

'Opportunity is missed by most people because it
is dressed in overalls and looks like work'
—**Thomas Edison**

Approximately a year after the United Nations published its Sustainable Development Goals in 2015, the Business and Sustainable Development Commission estimated that achieving these SDGs will open up USD 12 trillion worth of market opportunities in just four areas—food and agriculture, cities, energy and materials and health and well-being. In addition, the implementation of SDGs could lead to nearly 380 million new jobs globally, with almost 90 per cent of them being in developing countries. The Commission argued that the pursuit of SDGs by businesses not only opens up new opportunities and unlocks big efficiency gains but also drives innovation and enhances reputation.[1] Further, it estimated that the first movers in aligning with these goals are likely to build a 5–15-year advantage.

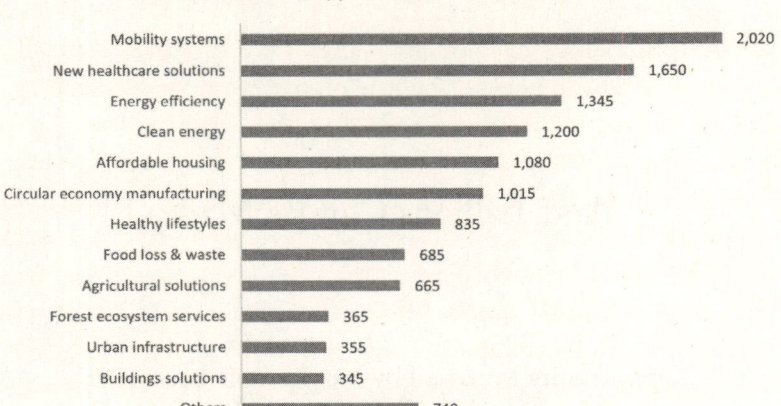

Value of incremental opportunities in 2030 (USD bn: 2015 values)

Mobility systems	2,020
New healthcare solutions	1,650
Energy efficiency	1,345
Clean energy	1,200
Affordable housing	1,080
Circular economy manufacturing	1,015
Healthy lifestyles	835
Food loss & waste	685
Agricultural solutions	665
Forest ecosystem services	365
Urban infrastructure	355
Buildings solutions	345
Others	740

Figure 3: Twelve largest business themes in a world economy heading for the global goals

Most of the SDGs involve serving unserved and underserved customers. There are often hidden advantages in figuring out solutions that work for such customers. One of the benefits that is easy to visualize but difficult to value is avoiding the increase in future competition from companies who figure out a way to address this segment. An often ignored and even harder to value benefit is the ability to open new demand from existing customers. How? Because any new product or service can be made equally appealing for existing customers. This will create new areas for both the company and the customer. A good example is Oxo peeler, a vegetable peeler which was built to address the needs of those with arthritis but proved to be a great product for regular users as well.

Sam Farber[2] founded Copco, a company specializing in tea kettles and cast iron cookware and sold it in 1982 at the age of fifty-eight. He then retired. A few years later, he and his wife, Betsey, spent a month in Southern France, cooking and enjoying the French countryside. One evening, while she was making dinner, his wife complained that the peeler was hurting her hands. Betsey had arthritis and she was flinching every time she used the peeler. She asked Sam if he could make the handle easier to hold, given that her husband had experience in kitchenware. That request stuck with him the whole evening. It kept Sam up the whole night, and finally, at half past one in the night, he rang Davin Stowell, the founder of Smart, a firm that had helped Sam with designing products for Copco. It was 7.30 p.m. in United States where Davin lived. He heard Sam's thoughts carefully and got to work on designing a better peeler. [3]

Eventually this led to the creation of the Oxo Swivel peeler with rubber handle, which was better for everyone to use—not just those with arthritis. In fact, it became one of the most sold peelers of all time. Nearly three decades after its release, it maintains a 4.8 star rating out of 5 on Amazon. Today, the kitchen brand Oxo is a favourite with customers—and it's all thanks to Sam's desire to help his wife, coupled with Davin's innovation at creating a new peeler design.

Designing for extreme customers is a core principle for many designers worldwide. In recent times, Nike has emerged as a great example of how addressing the needs of previously overlooked customers can unlock large potential markets. In 2012, Matthew Walzer, a sixteen-year-old with cerebral palsy, contacted Nike. He wrote, 'At 16 years old, I am able to completely dress myself, but my parents still have to tie my shoes. As a teenager who is striving to become totally self-sufficient, I find this extremely frustrating and, at times, embarrassing.' He told Nike that it was his dream to go to college without worrying about someone having to tie his shoelaces every day. Nike studied his case carefully. As a baby, Matthew was born two months prematurely, with underdeveloped lungs. The lack of oxygen supply to his brain had led to cerebral palsy. Matthew could do many things as a sixteen-year-old, but tying his own shoelaces was a challenge. Designing for his needs led to the development of Nike Go FlyEase—a range of no-lace footwear designed in 2015 that became a hit with everyone because of the ease of use. [4]

I am not trying to change the topic to design thinking. These examples show that extreme customers, defined as those that are difficult to address, can help us unlock new opportunities. This is exactly what addressing SDGs could offer businesses—an opportunity to address the needs of unserved and underserved customers. This could potentially unlock massive hidden value. Therefore, businesses should actively seek out these challenges rather than avoid them. Not surprisingly, the returns from solving for sustainability have also demonstrated value in this opportunity as we discuss in the next section.

4

Early Trends Are Positive

'In God we trust. All others must bring data'
—W. Edwards Deming

Any conversation on investing is accompanied by discussion on performance, and rightly so. The objective of investing is to generate returns. If commercial capital is to focus on addressing sustainable development goals, strong investment performance, especially superior relative performance compared to other available options—is crucial. The SDGs came into effect only in 2015 and the word 'impact investing' was coined around 2007–08. Hence, the overall industry is very new. As a result, it's hard to prove long-term performance, but what is very clear is that the early trends are very promising.

Morgan Stanley Institute for Sustainable Investing in its annual performance review report stated that sustainable funds outperformed their traditional peers in 2023 with a median return of 12.6 per cent compared to traditional funds' 8.6 per cent, according to Morningstar data.[1] The analysis was done on 97,000 funds globally, including closed-end funds, exchange-traded funds and open-end funds. However, what was particularly notable was that this outperformance spanned asset classes and geographies.

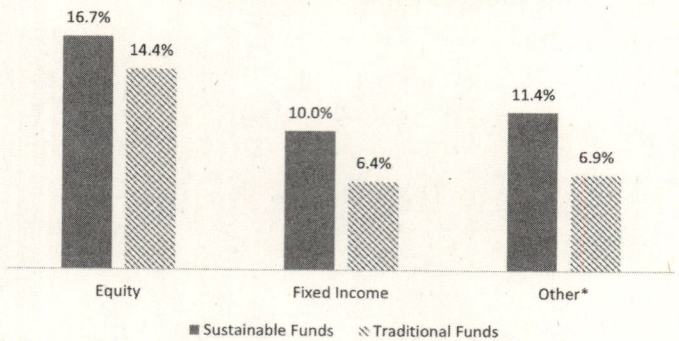

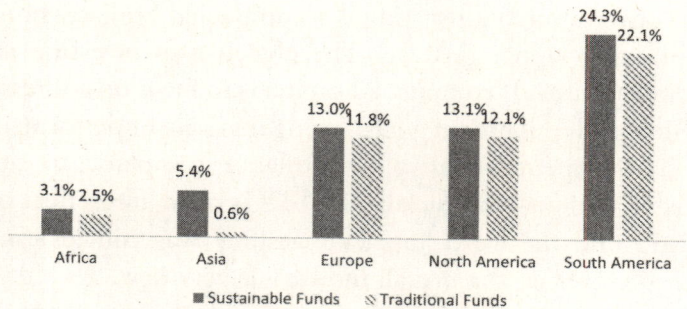

Figure 4: Sustainable funds outperformed across all asset classes and major geographies

Even when we look at long term data from the beginning of 2019, it is very clear that sustainable funds have continued to outperform traditional funds. A USD 100 investment in sustainable funds at the end of December 2018 would have grown to USD 135 by the end of December 2023, whereas the same amount invested in traditional funds would have been worth USD 125 over the same period. If we look at half-yearly performance of these funds since 2019, except for a one-year period between July 2021 and June 2022, sustainable funds have consistently outperformed traditional funds, as shown in the chart below.

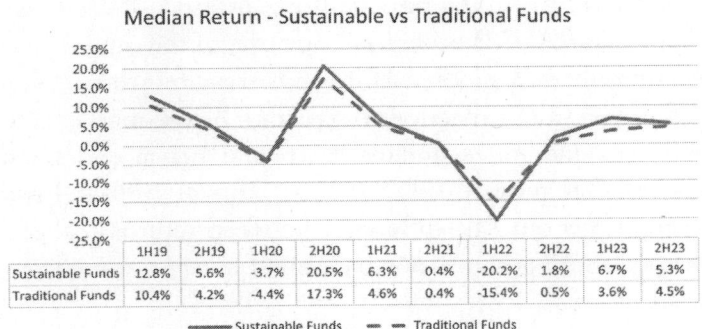

	1H19	2H19	1H20	2H20	1H21	2H21	1H22	2H22	1H23	2H23
Sustainable Funds	12.8%	5.6%	-3.7%	20.5%	6.3%	0.4%	-20.2%	1.8%	6.7%	5.3%
Traditional Funds	10.4%	4.2%	-4.4%	17.3%	4.6%	0.4%	-15.4%	0.5%	3.6%	4.5%

Median Return - Sustainable vs Traditional Funds

Sustainable Funds — — Traditional Funds

Figure 5: Sustainable funds have consistently outperformed traditional funds

This outperformance was, in a way, anticipated by Cambridge Associates—one of the world's largest investment firms—when it stated in its 2020 paper, 'The Materiality of Sustainability for Investors': 'Sustainability trends are mispriced because investors tend to have short-time horizons, behavioural biases and an over-reliance on history that is less relevant in the face of issues like a changing climate.' The report refers to several studies that provide support that sustainability trends were already having a tangible impact on asset performance in private markets, public equities and even in index investing.

One important parameter to consider while looking at the performance of sustainable and impact investing is that some part of the capital invested for impact has concessionary return expectations with philanthropy also categorized under impact. However, a large part of the capital focused on impact expects to generate commercial returns. Global Impact Investing Network (GIIN), in its 2023 report[2] titled GIINSIGHT states that 74 per cent of the impact investors surveyed were looking for risk-adjusted market returns while another 14 per cent of the impact investors were looking for returns closer to market-rate. The balance 12 per cent of the investors were looking for returns closer to capital preservation. In terms of assets under management (AUM) though, a large part of the capital is likely to be from investors looking for commercial returns.

The investors expecting to generate below market returns usually provide concessionary terms and hence end up with below market returns. GIIN's 2020 Annual Impact Investor Survey brings out this difference between returns realized by investors offering concessionary capital and those focusing on market returns.

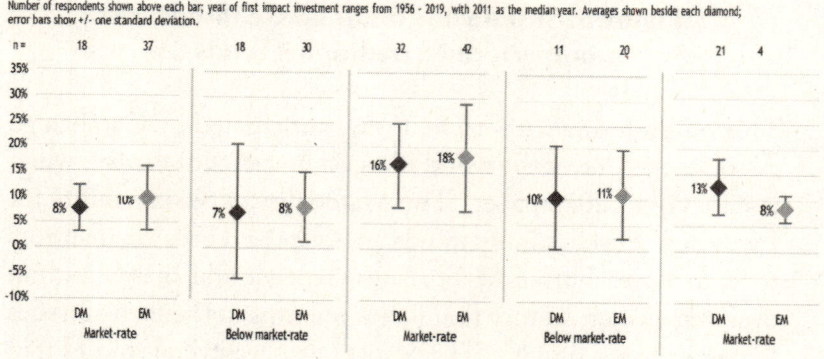

Number of respondents shown above each bar; year of first impact investment ranges from 1956 - 2019, with 2011 as the median year. Averages shown beside each diamond; error bars show +/- one standard deviation.

Figure 6: Average realized gross returns since inception for private markets investments[3]

Source: Global Impact Investing Network (GIIN), 'Annual Impact Investor Survey 2020: Executive Summary', [date], https://s3.amazonaws.com/giin-web-assets/giin/assets/publication/research/giin-annual-impact-investor-survey-2020-executive-summary.pdf

In this book, when we use the word impact investors, we consider investors who focus on delivering market-rate returns while delivering impact. Hence, the trends to focus on are the returns generated by impact investors who focus on generating market-rate returns and this is extremely positive.

The biennial survey done by Cambridge Associates has seen a consistent increase in institutions actively engaged in sustainable and impact investing from 36 per cent in 2018 to 61 per cent in 2020 and 65 per cent in 2022. The survey also points out that more than half of the institutions engaged in sustainable and impact investing allocate more than 5 per cent of their portfolio to sustainable and impact investments and more than a quarter allocate over 25 per cent.[4] As more capital gets allocated to sustainable and impact investing, the increase in flows is likely to drive returns for those who have backed the trends early. Given that the allocation to sustainable and impact investing is still very nascent, there is a long runway ahead.

5

What Is Impact Investing?

'One of the myths we're still debunking is that investing
in impact is by definition concessionary from a return
perspective. We need to show that when you invest well—
with a strong impact methodology and understanding of the
sectors and types of companies you're investing in—you can
find opportunities in which the business itself drives great
financial returns, which in turn drives impact'
**—Maya Chorengel, managing partner of
The Rise Fund in *Maya Chorengel
on building the impact investing industry*[1]**

I spent ten years in private equity before transitioning to a firm
specializing in impact investments. While I had heard about
impact investing and knew some of the firms in the market,
I always assumed that the impact investors have access to
concessionary capital and are not chasing market rate returns.
However, as I was evaluating the opportunity to take up the
role in impact investing, I understood that most of the impact
investors raise capital from third party investors and promise
market rate returns to their investors. And if they are not able
to generate those returns, they will not be able to raise capital
in future. Some philanthropies and concessionary capital

providers do get clubbed as impact investors; however, a large number of the impact investors are chasing commercial market-rate returns.

There is a lot of confusion on the difference between Environmental, Social and Governance (ESG) and impact investing. When I first told a friend of mine that I am considering writing a book on impact investing, he thought it was not a good idea. When I tried to dive deeper as to why he felt so, he said, 'Elon Musk is against it. Who is going to read your book?' I could then connect the dots that he was referring to the tweets made by Elon Musk about ESG ratings when he felt that Tesla's ESG ratings were unfairly poor.

Figure 7: Elon Musk's tweets on ESG

Sources: X (formerly Twitter), Elon Musk, https://x.com/elonmusk/status/1526957672200908801 and https://x.com/elonmusk/status/1526958110023245829

These tweets on 19 May 2022 came immediately after S&P excluded Tesla from its ESG index, citing concerns over the company's management, workplace conditions and its handling of an investigation into deaths and injuries linked to its driver-assistance systems. Tesla was also criticized for their codes of business conduct, racial discrimination, poor working conditions and the lack of a low carbon-strategy.[4] ESG funds were attracting large sums of money, and Tesla's exclusion from the list meant that those funds would not be able to include Tesla in their portfolio. This exclusion was likely to reduce the demand for Tesla stock and impact their share prices, and in effect, Elon Musk's wealth.

Three days later, on 22 May 2022, Morningstar published an article titled 'This is why Tesla's ESG Rating isn't Great'.[5] Sustainalytics, a sustainability data and analytics firm owned by Morningstar, gave Tesla a Medium ESG Risk Rating, citing weak product governance and other issues. The article quotes Jon Hale, director of sustainability for the Americas at Sustainalytics, stating, 'Tesla makes a product that will clearly help us transition to a low-carbon economy, but the company does have other issues of concern to ESG investors in its product governance, labour relations, a racial discrimination suit, and corporate governance.' It also quotes Driss Lembachar, who follows Tesla for Sustainalytics, stating, 'A big chunk of Tesla's success is its reputational capital, as a company that helps with the climate problem. Exclusions from indices highlight other problems on the social and governance side that may damage the reputational moat, or reputational capital.'

Elon Musk's frustration is understandable in the context that Tesla is part of the solution to one of the biggest problems of our time. The overarching solution to climate change, proposed by Bill Gates in his book *How to Avoid a Climate Disaster*, is to replace everything from fossil fuels to electricity and focus on generating electricity through clean energy. Electrifying transportation, which contributes 16 per cent of the overall 52 billion tons of greenhouse gas emissions,[6] is an important part of the solution. Tesla had already made a huge contribution by pushing the world in the direction of electric cars. Musk's tweets about fossil fuel and tobacco companies being rated high on ESG ratings shone the spotlight on one of the key aspects of ESG ratings—that they had been prepared with investment risks in mind, since they focus on the impact that ESG issues could have on company performance and not the impact those companies have on environment and their stakeholders. As a result, companies such as ExxonMobil, which is one of the largest oil and gas companies, got higher ratings as long as they were taking progressive steps on social and governance matters since the perceived impact of environment on their business was low even though they were impacting the environment significantly. This is a serious concern since the clients allocating money to the funds, that focused on ESG, believed that they were investing in companies which would not harm the environment while the ESG ratings rated companies such as Exxon high on that list because their financial performance is not likely to be impacted because of ESG factors, even though the primary activity of these businesses harms the environment.

ESG Is About Not Doing Anything Bad

To understand Tesla's situation better, let's step back and try to understand what ESG is in the first place. ESG is about not doing anything bad from environmental, social and governance perspective. In the private investing world, ESG analysis has existed for a very long time. I have been monitoring ESG performance of our portfolio companies even before I started in the impact investing world. The methodology was simple—

assess the impact that the company has on the environment, how the company treats its stakeholders, especially its employees and how the company's systems and processes ensure shareholder rights are protected. We create a checklist of all the items related to these factors and then assess how the company's performance and policies measure up against them. Based on the assessment, we might choose not to invest in the company if there are serious concerns. Even in case we invest, we develop a plan to continue to improve the company along environment, social and governance parameters. As an investor, the ESG information is also used to assess investment risk. For instance, if you discover that the company is not complying with some of the environmental norms which you expect could become laws in future, then you know that you run the risk if you invest in the company. However, private market investors primarily focus on assessing the company's impact on the environment and stakeholders. This is different to the way ESG ratings which focused primarily on assessing investment risks and the potential impact on the company's financial performance from environmental, social and governance aspects. As pointed in an article by SocialSuite,[7] 'MSCI, the largest ESG rating company, doesn't even try to measure the impact of a corporation on the world. It's all about whether the world might mess with the bottom line.'

In the public markets, investors cannot influence their investee companies to the extent that private market investors do. As investors started focusing on ESG matters, rating agencies developed scorecards to help investors understand these parameters. A large part of this work involved assessing the risk from ESG factors on the company rather than the impact that the company has on the environment and its stakeholders. Bloomberg had brought this out in an article in Dec 2021,[8] in which they pointed out the absurdity of good ESG ratings for McDonald's, which is one of the largest purchasers of beef, a critical contributor to greenhouse emissions.[9]

Musk's tweets did help in making the world more aware of what ESG ratings meant. A change was definitely needed to make sure that common people allocating to ESG funds do not invest hoping that the companies that they are investing in are actually impacting the environment positively. Not surprisingly, it led to changes in the ESG rating world. Several large rating agencies disclosed their mechanism for ESG ratings and some of them also decided to change it to incorporate the impact of companies on environment, social and governance aspects. Moody's refined their ESG assessment methodology to incorporate the impacts of the businesses being rated on the environments and societies they operate.[10] S&P announced in August 2023 that it will scrap ESG credit indicators.[11]

Impact Investing Is about Doing Good

Impact investing goes way beyond ESG. The term impact investing was coined in mid-2000s by a group of investors, entrepreneurs and philanthropists assembled by The Rockefeller Foundation.[12] In nearly fifteen years since then, impact investing has scaled up to become a USD 2.3 trillion industry.[13] For a large part of these fifteen years, it has remained a loosely defined term with significant flexibility in interpretation. Impact investing is about doing good. An impact investor picks a cause or causes that they would like to make a difference towards and then works towards identifying and making investments that are aligned with those goals. In that sense, it avoids the generic pitfalls and external benchmarks of ESG approach. It is not about avoiding negative impacts but making a positive impact.

International Finance Corporation (IFC) defined impact investing in its 2019 report titled 'Creating Impact: The Promise of Impact Investing'. According to this definition, impact investments are 'investments made in companies or organizations with the intent to contribute measurable positive social or environmental impact, alongside a financial return'. IFC identifies three attributes that are essential for an investment to be termed as 'Impact Investment'.

They are:

- **Intent** to achieve a social or environmental goal by identifying outcomes that will be pursued through the investment and specifying who will benefit from these outcomes.
- **Contribution** made by the investor for achievement of the intended goal. Contribution could be financial or non-financial.
- **Measurement** of improvement in social and environmental outcomes delivered by the enterprise into which the investment has been made.

The below schematic made by IFC summarizes this well:

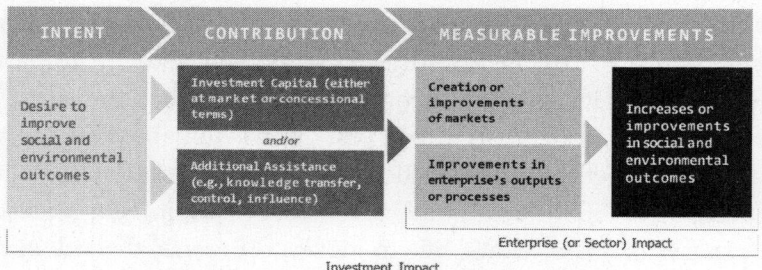

Figure 8: Summary of impact investing by IFC

Source: IFC, 'Investing for Impact', 2021, page 20, Figure 2.1, https://www.ifc.org/content/dam/ifc/doc/mgrt/2021-investing-for-impact-fin2.pdf

Let's understand each of these attributes a bit better.

Intent

The investors are at liberty to define the intended area of impact (e.g. Education, Health, Inclusion etc.) or intended beneficiaries (e.g. emerging markets, developed markets, specific country/state/community). In addition to this, most investors have moved over time towards identifying their initiatives with one or more of the seventeen Sustainable Development Goals (SDGs) developed by United Nations.[14] According to GIINSIGHT,[15] a report published by Global Impact Investing Network in 2023, 76 per cent of the impact investors use SDGs as one of the frameworks guiding impact strategy.

Contribution

Contribution is defined as the difference that the investor makes to the firm or the market. It is essentially the value added by the investor that helps improve societal or environmental outcomes. The investor can add value in three ways:

- Financial Contribution: Providing capital over and above the investment is usually considered as a contribution. However, the financial investment itself can be considered as contribution in case it is subsidized and/or offered to projects which do not have any other source of funding.
- Knowledge and Technical Assistance: Impact investors, especially in private markets, can provide knowledge and technical assistance, similar to that provided by venture capital and private equity firms to their investees.
- Influence or Control of Management: Influencing management of the company by incorporating covenants in agreements, driving decisions as a director on the board, proactive engagement as a shareholder or using your own team/consultants to provide hands-on management.

Private investments are more likely to meet these criteria than public investments, as they are primarily directed into the company rather than being secondary transactions in listed companies, where investors typically buy shares from other shareholders. This direct investment enables the company to allocate capital towards achieving its impact objectives. Also, private investors have more say in the functioning of the company, as representatives on the board and through shareholder agreements, that allows them to contribute towards impact outcomes. As a result, the contribution is more tangible in private investments when compared with the contribution by investors in public market investments.

Measurement

Measurement is critical to ensure alignment to the outcomes initially envisaged. However, given the multitude of factors involved there is no standard way of measuring impact. There are a few guidelines that can help in measuring the impact outcomes. One of them is the 'Five Dimensions' framework developed by Impact Management Project, a time bound forum of several practitioners for building global consensus on how to measure, assess and report impacts on people and the natural environment.

Impact dimension	Description
What	What tells us what outcome the enterprise is contributing to, whether it is positive or negative, and how important the outcome is to the people and communities experiencing it, as well as to the planet.
Who	Who describes the people and communities experiencing the outcome across multiple characteristics such as gender, class, race, sexual orientation, and Indigenous status, and explores differences in outcomes based on these characteristics and / or unique intersections of these characteristics.
How Much	How Much tells us how many people experienced the outcome, what degree of change they experienced, and how long they experienced the outcome.
Contribution	Contribution tells us whether an enterprise's efforts resulted in outcomes that were likely better than what likely would have occurred otherwise.
Risk	Risk tells us the likelihood that impact will be different than expected.

Figure 9: IMP's five dimensions for measuring impact

Source: Impact Frontiers, 'Five Dimensions of Impact', https:// impactfrontiers.org/norms/five-dimensions-of-impact/

As we will notice later in conversations with investors, each of them has developed their own framework on measuring impact. Impact measurement provides proof of impact and hence is the critical backbone of impact investing. The objective of impact measurement is to ensure that you are assessing what you set out to achieve and, by definition, will vary for investors with different objectives.

Operating Principles for Impact Management

In addition to defining the key attributes of impact investment, IFC has developed in partnership with several impact asset managers 'Operating Principles for Impact Management',[16] which can be used by the investors to demonstrate the impact achieved through their investments. As of Jan 2021, there are 151 signatories to these principles. One of the key reasons for defining impact investing and building operating principles is to avoid 'Impact Washing' (falsely labeling funds as impact funds) or 'Greenwashing' (intentionally exaggerating or misrepresenting sustainability characteristics) by asset managers. One of the most recent events around Greenwashing involved Deutsche Bank controlled investment firm DWS, which has assets under management of Euro 963 billion,[17] and was raided by German authorities in May 2022.[18] It later agreed to pay USD 25 million to U.S. Securities and Exchange Commission (SEC) to settle charges over these matters. Hence, ensuring compliance with operating principles is important.

A brief overview of the nine operating principles is shown below. An independent third-party audit, which is one of the key requirements under operating principles, is expected to reduce impact washing and improve the authenticity of impact asset managers.

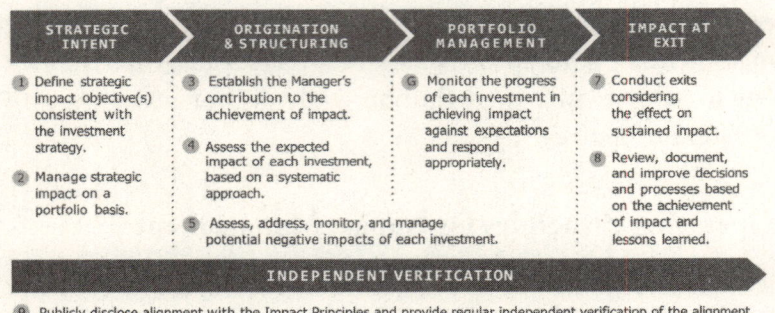

Figure 10: Operating principles of impact management

Source: International Finance Corporation (IFC), 'Investing for Impact', 2021, p. 29, https://www.ifc.org/content/dam/ifc/doc/mgrt/2021-investing-for-impact-fin2.pdf

I do not intend to bore you with the definitions and theory of impact investing because, at its core, it's quite simple. Identify an area where you want to make a difference, invest in companies that align with the cause, contribute to it and measure your success. The best way to understand impact investing would be to see how the leading and successful practitioners of impact investing go about it.

The second section of the book has eight chapters, each dedicated to one investor. Some of these investors have been investing for impact from even before the word 'impact' was coined. More importantly, each one of them has generated strong returns. These investors have been chosen to ensure that, in this book, we cover private equity investors, attempting to address various challenges, from climate change to financial inclusion, across various geographies, including emerging and developed countries, and invest across various stages—from early-stage ventures to established traditional companies. This demonstrates the opportunity that lies ahead of us across sectors and geographies.

Part 2

The Secrets of H.I.T. Investors

6

AC Ventures: Empowering MSMEs in Indonesia Through e-Commerce and Financial Services

In 1998, Adrian Li took a gap year before going to university. He decided to spend much of that year backpacking through rural China. The plan was to start from the south, move through Tibet and then travel west to Xinjiang, before finally making his way back to Beijing. It would be the kind of trip that changed his life forever. It was an interesting time to be travelling through China for a curious young man. The country was coming off the convocation of the fifteenth Party Congress, and the year 1998 had started with reforms moving ahead full steam. Politically, this manifested in a palpable relaxation of the intellectual atmosphere, the adoption of a major plan for reorganizing the State Council at the March meeting of the National People's Congress (NPC), and the acceleration of the restructuring of state-owned enterprises (SOEs). In the summer of that year, however, reform was visibly slowing down. The impact of the Asian financial crisis, discontent among laid-off workers, heightened concerns over corruption and smuggling, and new challenges from democracy activists led to progress taking two steps backwards. Moreover, domestic reform was supported by an active program of diplomacy, including a

41

state visit by US President Bill Clinton and a series of summit meetings in Asia.[1] For Li, travelling through rural China was an eye-opener. That year, China suffered the worst floods in over forty-four years. The central and southern parts of the country along the banks of the Yangtze River and its tributaries were battered by more than sixty days of heavy flooding. In July and August, extensive flooding also occurred in the northeast, along the Songhuajiang, Nenjiang and other rivers. According to governmental estimates, 223 million people—one-fifth of China's population were affected, 3004 people died and fifteen million were made homeless. Fifteen million farmers lost their crops. The floods caused severe damage to critical facilities such as health clinics, schools, water supply and other infrastructure such as roads, bridges and irrigation systems as well as industrial facilities. At the end of August, direct economic damage was estimated at over USD 20 billion.[2] The damage was on widespread display as Li travelled through China's rural heartlands. The floods had only served to deepen the poverty that marked the interiors of China and Tibet. In fact, one of the moments that stuck with him was an encounter with a group of homeless children in Tibet. As Li watched, one of the kids, who was scrabbling in the rubbish to find food, sliced his finger on the serrated edges of a half-open can. Li would never forget that image. He knew then that something needed to be done to provide prosperity for people everywhere.

Years later, during his last year at Cambridge, he founded a society that ran a charity event, with all the proceeds being used to support a charity called Project Hope in China. Project Hope was a government-established charity to support the education of underprivileged children. Adrian's parents had brought him up with the belief that education was the equalizer that society needed. It provided new opportunities and opened up new vistas for those with potential. He would always continue supporting Project Hope, via events and marathons in support of the cause.

During his MBA at Stanford, he worked alongside another co-founder on building an online platform in China to teach English. He spent the final year of his degree working on the business plan through a start-up course that was offered. Eventually, his efforts met with success, and he received the funding he wanted in the summer of 2006. After graduating, Adrian passed on a very lucrative job offer with an attractive sign on bonus from one of the largest consumer companies and moved to China, where he used his funding to build Idapted, the edtech company he had been thinking about for a long time. The company focused on teaching English speaking skills to students online, in a high-quality, scalable and effective way. Idapted used the Internet to connect English learners in China to teachers in native English-speaking countries, such as the United States of America.

For Idapted, getting teachers in the USA was easy. Driven by the success of Liveops, the world's largest virtual call center, which was bringing call center work back home from countries like India and the Philippines, people in the USA had grown accustomed to such models. However, getting students in China to go online for learning English-speaking skills was not that straightforward. The need for this service was apparent—many Chinese students had studied English for years, but were unable to communicate or speak fluently, limiting their economic and educational potential.

In 2006, if you recall, mobile networks ran on 2G. Students in China were not looking for online English-speaking courses, and hence, it required significant offline marketing effort. Adrian and his co-founder established their office in a residential apartment directly across from one of China's largest universities. They distributed leaflets and walked interested students to an internet café, where they had blocked a few desktops for Idapted, so that students could take their lessons. They also fine-tuned the program so that they could help these students score better on tests such as TOEFL. Despite the challenges in accessing courses online, thousands of students were still paying for their service. Adrian and his co-founder scaled the company, raising a couple of rounds of venture financing. However, they ultimately sold the business to a US company named Eleutian.

Eleutian used Skype for one-to-many teaching in Japanese and Korean markets. Idapted's technology and market entry into China proved valuable to Eleutian. This was Adrian's first entrepreneurial experience, and it was a fulfilling one. It brought together many of the things that he hoped technology would eventually achieve, though the timing was perhaps a bit ahead of the curve. A few years after Adrian had sold Idapted, a company named VIPKid, which offered services similar to those of Idapted, emerged in China and became a unicorn.

Adrian had an exit, albeit not a material one. Shortly afterwards, he happened to meet Oliver Samwer at Rocket Internet. Inspired by the dot-com boom, Oliver Samwer and his brothers Alexander and Marc created a German auction site, Alando, in 1999 and sold it to eBay for USD 43 million after a few months. That was followed by the creation of mobile phone content provider Jamba! which they sold to Verisign in 2004 for USD 273 million. Thereafter, they founded Berlin-based tech incubator Rocket Internet in 2007 and took it public in October 2014. The fundamental idea was a simple one: to copy business models proven in the US or China and adapt them to high-potential markets outside those two countries, grow fast and sell the business at an attractive price. Adrian was fascinated with Oliver's idea of taking proven innovation and timing the market entry of a product or service to catch up with markets. It made sense to him because the model wasn't about innovation, but rather bringing proven innovation and localizing it to markets where it hadn't existed yet. Oliver had done this many times over, building businesses and selling them. Adrian worked with Rocket Internet, initially in China, to build an Airbnb type of business and he learnt how quickly a company could scale, with good timing involved. He built this business from zero to 200 employees in six months, with 6,00,000 nights booked through the platform.

Just before joining Rocket Internet, Adrian met Vanessa, whom he would later marry, through the Entrepreneurs' Organization (EO) in Beijing. She was from Indonesia, and when he visited the country to see her, the businessman in him was blown away by the potential of the Indonesian market. At that time, i.e. around 2010–2011, there were barely any e-commerce marketplaces or online travel agents and no ride hailing businesses. There were just a handful of local media players, such as Viva and Kaskus, along with global tech businesses, such as Google and Facebook. Knowing what he knew and having experienced what he had in China, he felt he had an edge to bring these types of proven innovations or technology-enabled business models to Indonesia. So, he moved with Rocket Internet to Indonesia and played a part in building an e-commerce business. A year and a half after moving to Indonesia, a classmate from Stanford GSB introduced him to one of the large conglomerates in Indonesia. It was at this point that he got the opportunity to start a fund.

Adrian Starts Convergence Ventures

Many of the conglomerates in Indonesia are built on traditional businesses such as natural resources, commodities or trading. They all recognized that their businesses would be disrupted by new technologies but did not know how to get involved. One of the ways to do that was to invest. Through several conversations, one of these conglomerates decided to anchor the fund for Adrian. They knew quite a few other conglomerates, and Adrian raised more capital from them, as well as from some entrepreneurs and investors in China. He believed that there were clear opportunities to serve large segments of the population who are underprivileged, and the democratizing power of technology could improve their livelihoods.

As he did more work and understood what the opportunities were, the thesis of the fund started coalescing primarily around three areas:

a) Commerce and its derivatives: Online commerce has an accessibility effect that allows people to enjoy the benefits of living in a more developed city, regardless of where they are located.

b) Financial services: Even though some of the banks were the largest companies in South-east Asia, over 80 per cent of the population was unbanked or underbanked. This presented a huge opportunity because, without access to financial products, consumers and businesses are highly limited.

c) Micro small and medium enterprises (MSMEs): MSMEs account for 63 per cent of Indonesia's economy by GDP and employ close to 90 per cent of the workforce in the country. This sector is a massive engine of growth, but there are a lot of inefficiencies in these businesses. Many MSMEs are underbanked and need to get into online commerce to distribute their products.

Adrian believed that these were the sectors which were large and where technology will have a massive role to play in disrupting the traditional ways of doing business.

Adrian named his firm Convergence Ventures and began working on Fund I, with a focus on online commerce, financial services and MSMEs, in 2014. They started making investments at the tail end of 2014 after raising initial capital. The final close for Fund I happened in 2016 at USD 30 million. The fund was valued at just over 3.2x MOIC[3] resulting in around 30 per cent IRR.[4]

Julo: Credit Card for the Unbanked

One of the major successes of Fund I was Julo, a company that provides a revolving credit facility—similar to a credit card—for low- and middle-income consumers in Indonesia. This allows consumers to fund cash emergencies for personal purposes, such as health and education or business purposes such as working capital and capital expenditure. It was founded by Adrianus Hitijahubessy, an Indonesian who had completed his master's in Machine Learning and Artificial Intelligence from the University of Texas in 2006. Hitijahubessy had joined Capital One as an analyst. Capital One was a consumer credit card company which focused on the sub-prime segment. According to Hitijahubessy, his job had nothing to do with his education. However, it was his experience in data and risk analytics that would provide the foundation for his future as the founder of Julo. From there, he transitioned to eBay, focusing on product and finance analytics, before moving to Cignifi, where he leveraged alternative data to develop credit scores and gain insights into customer attributes such as loyalty and fraud propensity. Hitijahubessy was pleased. He felt that he was finally using his academic skills in machine learning. It was here that he realized that these models—the same ones that were being developed for Brazil, Mexico and other Latin American countries—were also likely to work in Indonesia. He believed that the market opportunity in Indonesia was huge, especially given that 70 per cent of the people were either underbanked or unbanked.

In 2016, Adrianus decided to come back to Indonesia and set up a lending firm, which leveraged alternative data to offer credit to unbanked and underbanked consumers. He convinced Hans Sebastian, who had also studied in the United States and had also worked with leading software firms such as Siemens and Mozilla, to join him in this mission. And thus, Julo was born.

In hindsight, the timing for Julo was just right. Indonesia had just introduced P2P lending regulations in 2016. If they had started earlier, the idea would have been ahead of its time, and in the absence of a proper regulatory framework, it would have been tough going, to say the least. And yet, if they had been delayed by a couple of years, there would have been more competition.

Adrianus was one of the rare founders in fintech in Indonesia who possessed the vision and experience that was highly relevant for someone like Adrian Li. It wasn't long before he bought into the plan that Hans and Adrianus had for the future. In their opinion, the primary reason that incumbents, such as banks and other financial services firms, were not able to tap into the unbanked and underbanked segment was because of the lack of data. In the absence of data, assessing a customer would require significant effort. For loans of USD 100, for instance, that effort really didn't make economic sense. But Adrianus believed that alternative data could be used to predict customer behaviour. It wasn't hard to build such models. It was something that most data scientists were easily able to do, but the true test of such models lay in their real-world performance.

Over time, Julo developed a model that calculated three scores, which they termed ABC: A stands for Application score, which captures alternative data for a new user; B stands for Behaviour score, which captures how the customer behaves once the loan is approved and C stood for Collection data, which captures repayment data. Julo makes initial assessment based on alternative data such as their profession, type of mobile phone used and the residential address and use of funds shared by the clients, most of whom do not have a credit track record. However, the real innovation introduced by Julo was in 2018—when they launched a revolving credit line, similar to a credit card for their customers. Essentially, once approved, the customers had access to their credit limit forever.

While Julo does not mandate that loans be solely used for productive purposes, the top four reasons for borrowing— business expansion or working capital challenges, education financing, home renovation and improvement and healthcare— account for more than two-thirds of all loans. Julo believes in supporting customers through their life journey. The performance of Julo's credit engine has been so good that they have been able to sell it as a solution to other large clients, such as Grab, one of the largest tech companies in Indonesia, with presence in ride-hailing across South-east Asia.

Julo has continuously innovated to serve the needs of its customers. In January 2023, for instance, it launched seminars to improve financial literacy among its clients. In March 2023, Julo enabled its digital credit service to be used directly for payment of fees for school, tuition and vocational courses in more than 2,50,000 educational institutes across Indonesia. In August 2023, it revamped its onboarding process to offer digital credit limit in just five minutes to new customers. In December 2023, it started embedding insurance protection in its products. And in January 2024, it enabled payments to nearly 25,000 health facilities across Indonesia.

Convergence was one of the first investors in Julo, investing USD 50,000 in 2017. This was followed by a USD 5,00,000 investment in the middle of 2018. Adrian and his team at Convergence worked closely with Julo's founders and helped them at several stages. At the beginning, they guided them on regulatory processes and assisted in navigating the process for obtaining a P2P lending license. They also helped Julo reach out to the right investors that helped in attracting reputed investors in south-east Asia such as Quona, Gobi, Saratoga and Credit Saison. Adrian and his team also helped Julo raise debt from Credit Saison. Most recently, they helped in reaching out to regulators and voicing their concerns on certain aspects. On the back of this support, Julo has been able to serve millions of unbanked and underbanked individuals. It disbursed more than USD 454 million in 2023 and achieved an annual recurring revenue of USD 120 million by the end of 2023.

Merger of Equals: Agaeti and Convergence Combine to Become AC Ventures

One of Adrian's classmates from Stanford GSB, Pandu Sjahrir, had also established a similar fund for Indonesia named Agaeti Ventures together with Michael Soerijadji. They also delivered good returns of 3.5x MOIC[5] on a 2018 vintage fund. In 2019, Pandu and Adrian decided to work together and merged their firms to form AC Ventures (short for Agaeti Convergence). Together, they went back to the market and realized they had overlapping limited partners (LPs), who increased their exposure. When they raised the fund, they called it Fund III since the merger meant that there were already two funds—one each from Agaeti and Convergence. They began investing in 2019 and had the first close of Fund III in March 2020, just as Covid-19 started.

Although the COVID-19 pandemic left them with less capital than initially planned, they still found great investment opportunities at attractive valuations. The pandemic ensured that they took twice as long to do the final close for that fund. Still, they were able to raise USD 205 million for the fund, by the final close in 2021. Fund III continued to deliver strong performances and is rated amongst the top quartile performers in its vintage driven by investments such as Majoo.

Majoo: A Tech Enabler for MSMEs

Adi Rahadi, the founder of Majoo, joined Telkomsel, one of Indonesia's largest Telecom companies, after graduating as an electronics and communications engineer. He spent twenty-two years at Telkomsel, starting in IT department, moving on to strategy roles, and finally ending with a stint at Linkaja, where he led the mobile money business for micro enterprises. Even while working full time, Adi had a side gig selling POS (Point of Sale terminal) hardware to small business owners. This side gig made him realize the challenges faced by small business owners who manage everything end to end from sales to stock and accounts. He decided to build technological solutions that could help MSMEs run their operations more efficiently.

He reached out to a friend from his B-school days, Audia Harahap. He had been Adi's partner in a business plan competition, in which they had won the regional round representing their B-school in Bangkok, allowing them to advance to the final round at the University of Berkeley. Audia's experience as director of operations in his family business complimented Adi's skillsets. They started Majoo in 2019 and initially offered POS and cash management solutions. Over time, they developed a super app for small business owners that could help the owners digitize most business functions, including recording sales, managing inventory, handling employees, CRM and accounting.

Soon after starting, Majoo and the MSME segment it served were significantly impacted by COVID. When Majoo approached AC Ventures for funding, they were not convinced that Majoo would make it to the other side of the pandemic. Undaunted, Majoo used the opportunity to serve MSMEs, by helping them launch online businesses and address digital payments. When AC Ventures revisited the business later, they were pleasantly surprised by the uptick in the customer base. Now as confident as they had once been doubtful, AC Ventures backed Majoo with a USD 2.6 million investment in Q2 2021. Other investors, such as BRI Ventures and Xendit also joined the round, taking the overall amount raised to USD 4 million. They helped the company attract new investors, such as Quona and Hedosophia, for the next rounds, and increased their commitments during these rounds.

Majoo increased its customer base from 9000 MSMEs (before AC Ventures invested in 2021) to over 40,000 in less than three years. It also partnered with banks to offer loans to MSMEs by leveraging their data. Most recently, it started Majoo Supplies to help MSMEs source their inputs and raw materials conveniently in a cost-effective way. As a result, Majoo is expected to deliver strong returns for AC Ventures.

Backed by strong performance, AC Ventures closed its latest flagship fund in 2024 at USD 210 million, which is a huge achievement in a difficult fundraising environment. It had also launched a fund of USD 60 million focused on Malaysia in 2021, by partnering with the Malaysian Government. Recently, AC Ventures is launching a fund to focus on environment-related areas, such as energy transition and decarbonization, accounting for carbon footprints. AC Ventures believes that Indonesia, which is one of the most impacted countries because of climate change, has an important role to play in finding solutions. While they have already invested in some companies that are solving climate challenges, the fact that it is one of the most important challenges of our time and that the risk reward metrics of some of these investments are different warrant a dedicated fund.

Investment Strategy

AC Ventures invests from venture stage to growth equity. They aim to get a stake of 10–15 per cent with a flexible investment, which now starts at USD 5 million post the increase in fund size. They closely look at ideas that worked in the past. They try to understand highly compelling and proven internet or technology-enabled business models that have demonstrated traction and good unit economics from other parts of the world. After all, Indonesia is a catch-up market. Adrian believes that, given its demographics, it is probably one of the last large markets in the world, which is catching up with India and China.

The key initial filter questions for AC Ventures are: is the market big enough? Is this the right timing? Is this a model that we understand?

They are open to investing in new models but focus on gaining a deeper understanding of the innovation risk. For example, AC Ventures invested in an agritech company that works closely with farmers by supporting them with agricultural inputs, best practices and streamlining the supply chain. This helps the farmers achieve better pricing and reduces end user costs, due to the reduction of inefficiencies.

Founder Evaluation Is Based on Qualitative and Quantitative Benchmarks from Prior Investments

Adrian believes that one of the most important factors in choosing the right company is founder quality. According to him, a lot of venture investors will emphasize this, but will not execute it as well as they talk about it. In his case, AC Ventures has done a fair bit of work retroactively, that they now apply on a forward-looking basis. This enables them to identify correlating factors and attributes that make for great teams. What does this mean, you might wonder? Simply put, for companies that are underperforming, they focus on identifying concrete quantitative factors—such as the number of founders and years of experience—alongside qualitative traits like strengths, leadership, execution capabilities and frugality. They assess these factors when they meet with the founders, and that becomes an important part of their evaluation matrix, which is used to decide on whether to back a company or not. They also conduct reference checks in addition to this.

The last piece of the evaluation process is traction. Some of the questions involved here are: have the companies achieved their targets to date? What are the numbers like? Are they trending up or down? AC Ventures has many benchmarks based on their extensive experience with numerous companies.

Impact Is a Critical Piece of the Puzzle

AC Ventures' portfolio companies have positively impacted over 7.5 million lives and businesses in the ASEAN region, including the improvement of lives for more than four million low-and middle-income earners and MSMEs. Around 61 per cent of their portfolio companies are present in second and third-tier cities, creating more than 2,00,000 jobs in the region. Additionally, they have empowered over 20,000 rural fishermen in some of the most economically vulnerable coastal communities, reflecting their commitment to meaningful change across different areas of society.[6]

All this was driven by a sharp focus on creating value. AC Ventures calculates net impact ratio across its portfolio by using The Upright Project, a software tool created by a technology company, based in Helsinki, Finland. The Upright Project measures ESG and impact according to Northern European standards. The 'net impact ratio' is a percentage score, used to quantify how effectively a group of companies turns resources into positive impact. Recently, ACV and its portfolio conducted baseline assessments across four key dimensions—environment, health, society and knowledge—achieving an above-average score of 37 percent, with society and health emerging as their strongest areas.[7]

Portfolio Allocation Strategy

The goal of AC Ventures is to capture higher returns, with lower loss ratios and lower volatility. They believe that optimal portfolio diversification happens at around thirty to thirty-five companies. A minimum ownership of 10 per cent to 15 per cent on the first cheques into these companies is their target. They reserve a two-to-one ratio for follow-on capital, rather than the standard one-to-one reserve. This approach enables them to be active deployers and decision-makers for follow-on cheques into the best companies, putting more money into those that demonstrate better traction and future potential than others.

Their philosophy is that the first investment in a company is riskier when evaluating a company from the outside, the entrepreneur is presenting their best case and there is never 100 per cent transparency. However, once they invest and work closely with the founder, they gain insight into their mistakes, learning, progress and personal growth, developing a high level of trust. This enables them to put an outsized follow-on cheque into the best companies, which AC Ventures believes provides them with an edge. The earlier they do this, the better, as the valuation of a great company only increases with time. However, they do not follow on for every single company equally.

For example, in a USD 250 million fund, they invest an average of USD 2 million per company in thirty to thirty-five companies, the total amount invested is USD 70 million, leaving nearly USD 140 million[8] for nearly twenty companies. This breaks down to roughly USD 7–8 million per company. Typically, in a fund, one-third of investments are written off, one-third are okay and around 20 per cent are real winners. However, by allocating more capital to follow-on investments in the existing portfolio, they concentrate more money on the winners.

Significant Focus on Value Creation

AC Ventures believes in a high level of involvement with their portfolio companies. They have ten people in the value creation team. In the West, the firm that really pioneered and championed this approach was Andreessen Horowitz, a private American venture capital firm, headquartered in Menlo, California. Founded in 2009, Andreessen Horowitz invests in both early-stage start-ups and established growth companies. Its investments span healthcare, consumer, cryptocurrency, gaming, fintech, education and enterprise IT (including cloud computing, security and software as a service) industries. The firm's partners work on behalf of all its portfolio companies, an approach modelled after the Hollywood talent agency, Creative Artists Agency.[9] However, this is not the usual approach in South-east Asia, where many firms have regional mandates, making it costly to build a team across the region. This is because every market has different regulators, companies and local market nuances that require building teams for every country. With AC Ventures' focus on Indonesia, they have been able to do it because every company they invest in operates in Indonesia. This also means that they have good synergies with regional investors. Entrepreneurs who want to expand in South-east Asia mostly want to start doing so in Indonesia, and they value hands-on support. AC Ventures offers support ranging from hiring a country manager to hosting events where entrepreneurs can connect with potential partners, making it a valuable ally for start-ups.

The firm's key pillars of value creation include talent operations, ESG, PR and communications, business development and deals to drive mergers and acquisitions (M&A), follow-on rounds and exits. The talent operations team provides support with everything from hiring and culture building to compensation benchmarking and scaling organizations. They offer standard playbooks and have experts available to provide training. The ESG team drives the necessary transformations across the portfolio. PR and communications assist with everything from crisis PR to fundraising announcements. Their business development team helps with key introductions for portfolio companies and creates networking events to connect them with the right people. They also assist with regulatory compliance and ensure that entrepreneurs know how to navigate the regulatory landscape. The fundraising team helps network with LPs[10] for co-investments, as well as other venture capital firms, and assists with potential M&A, follow-on rounds or exits.

Every quarter, the value creation team typically performs 50-60 key actions across the portfolio, and entrepreneurs receive an accountability email outlining all the actions that have been executed and items that are planned. The team also receives NPS[11] scores and suggestions for improvement. This comprehensive approach to value creation is a significant advantage for early-stage start-ups in Indonesia, where capable talent is scarce, and regulatory compliance can be complex.

The Scale Up of Start-Up Ecosystem Has Also Created More Exit Opportunities for Investors

As an early-stage investor, AC Ventures sells their stakes to late-stage investors or, in some cases, holds on till IPO. In fact, the IPO, as an exit option in Indonesia, has become real over the last decade. This is a development that has been incredibly valuable for early-stage investors, as it offers optionality. In turn, these public tech companies acquire other assets. In so doing, AC Ventures' portfolio companies have created market capitalization of over USD 7 billion.

When AC Ventures started investing, they believed that the most successful companies might only become unicorns (valued at or more than USD 1 billion). However, they have seen that the market has more potential. Sea Group was the first company to achieve this. Although they went through some turmoil after global expansion, they were still valued at USD 30 billion at their lowest point in the last 36 months. Since then, Grab and Gojek have also gone public, each being valued at USD 7–10 billion at their lowest. Additionally, other companies globally, such as the Indonesian e-commerce company Bukalapak, have also had successful local listings, even during a tough market in 2022.

Adrian believes that the best is yet to come. He says, 'We have many more companies that can go public in the future. As these public tech companies become self-sustaining, there will be a thriving acquisition market because no company can do everything itself. We saw a similar trend in the Chinese market where companies like Baidu, Alibaba, and Tencent initially tried to build everything themselves before acquiring other companies for their bolt-on acquisitions, talent hires, or talent acquisitions.' This is true even of large tech companies globally. For instance, most of Google's successful products after Search, including YouTube, Maps and Android, have been acquired. Meta has acquired Instagram and WhatsApp.

Outlook

Adrian believes that Indonesia is in a sweet spot due to various macro factors. South-east Asia is one of the most attractive demographic regions to invest in globally, and Indonesia, being the fourth largest country in the world by population, offers the most significant potential returns for venture investors. By 2050, Indonesia is expected to be the fourth-largest country in terms of GDP, which is an incredibly exciting prospect for investors.[12] Adrian says, 'When we look at the intersection of technology and digital consumption with the growth of the economy at large, we can see a clear path from 10 per cent penetration to 30 per cent penetration by the end of the decade, which represents a 3x growth opportunity. Another aspect to consider is where the capital is flowing. Geopolitical tensions and risks in Europe and the increasing rivalry between China and the US have created significant uncertainty for investors. As a result, even marginal additional capital flows from these markets to South-east Asia would represent a significant sum of money in this region.'

7

Apis Partners: Building a
Cashless Way to Inclusion

To this day, Matteo Stefanel, co-founder and CEO of Apis Partners, remembers tagging along with his grandmother when she visited the local coffee shop in their neighbourhood in Italy. Even though he was a kid in those days, he still remembers her order. She would always pay for two coffees, but she requested that only one coffee be given to her. It is part of an Italian tradition called *caffe sospeso*, which means 'suspended coffee'. That suspended coffee can be claimed by a poor person, who might want a free coffee. His grandmother's kindness towards total strangers always stayed with Stefanel. He was also influenced by his father, who would often provide free consultation on legal and accounting matters to people who might not be able to afford it otherwise.

The openness to the world and the integrity that Stefanel saw at home was reflected in the ideals of United World College (UWC), the college he attended when he was sixteen years old. UWC was founded on the principles of Kurt Hahn, a pioneer in education. Hahn had been deeply inspired by the cooperation and loyalty shown by military men, who had just come out of the bruising Second World War. His life had, thus far, been spent in the founding of a number of schools and educational organizations. In 1955, he saw education as a route to peace and the best way to ensure that compassion flowered in human society, especially after the horrors the world had seen during the war. It was in the kernels of these ideas that the UWC was born. Hahn was always deeply interested in the power of young minds. Education could seek to inspire connection, compassion and service, if directed properly. By the time Stefanel went to the UWC in Canada, the brand name was already a global voice for values and diversity-based education for peace and sustainability. Importantly, the UWCs worldwide placed a strong emphasis on diversity and its empowerment within specific national and cultural contexts. Students came from all over the world, and their presence—Stefanel's roommate was a Pakistani student—opened Stefanel's eyes to the challenges faced by emerging countries. Already greatly influenced by the values he had imbibed from his home life, Stefanel became convinced that his true calling lay in trying to make the world a better place.

He graduated in politics, philosophy and economics in 1997 and soon started a career in investment banking which eventually led to him joining Donaldson Lufkin & Jenrette (DLJ), one of the prominent investment banks in the US at that time, in 1999.[1] There, he met Udayan Goyal, his future co-founder, who joined DLJ around the same time. Given the long hours and challenges of working as associates in investment banking, the two became good friends.

Udayan followed a slightly different path to get into investment banking. As his father worked in the Indian Foreign Service (IFS), Udayan had grown up all over the world, moving to a new place every few years. He went to a boarding school in India at the age of eleven and then another boarding school in England at the age of sixteen. He studied immunology and genetic pathology at Cambridge University with the intent of entering the medical profession. However, once he completed his bachelor's degree, he felt that he wanted to work, rather than continue his medical studies. He joined Barclays' Capital before moving to DLJ, as an associate.

DLJ was acquired by Credit Suisse. After some time, Stefanel moved to Citigroup and then to Deutsche Bank in 2002. Here, he rose to become a managing director and the co-head of the Emerging Markets Financial Institutions Group. Udayan also moved to Deutsche Bank in 2005 and became the co-head of Financial Technology in Deutsche Bank's investment banking group.

In 2008, Matteo joined Abraaj, one of the prominent emerging market investors at that time, as a partner responsible for financial services. After spending five years with Abraaj, he decided to set up something on his own. With his extensive experience in financial services, and the fact that, globally speaking at that time, there were nearly 2.2 billion financially excluded people across the world, Stefanel was convinced that his skills would be best utilized to solve these challenges. It would be hard work and Stefanel was aware that it would be a long trek uphill.

Meanwhile, Udayan left Deutsche in 2009, and founded FT Advisors, a boutique advisory firm based in London, providing corporate finance and strategic advisory services to the financial technology sector. During this time, he started exploring ways in which he could contribute to society. While attending a TED event at the Infosys campus in India, he happened to meet Anand Shah, the founder of Sarvajal, which means 'water for all' in Sanskrit. Shah was working to create affordable access to clean drinking water in underserved areas across India. He had achieved this by financing and building plants in villages around the country. Customers were charged a very small volume-based fee, a nominal fee for the villagers themselves, though it was large enough to support the infrastructure and operations of the plant. In this way, it was commercially sustainable as well as impactful. Anand told Udayan that one of his major challenges was to collect the fees across the many touch points that existed. The two men innovated and came up with the idea of a pre-paid card. The experience opened Udayan's eyes to the potential of financial services in creating value. More importantly, it also helped him appreciate the value of profitability in ensuring sustainable impact.

So, when Matteo and Udayan set out to raise a fund in 2014, both were clear that they wanted their investments to create a meaningful impact—one that would remain sustainable only if it was backed by profitability. They named the firm Apis, which is Latin for bee, and which is representative of the role they felt that the firm could play as a pollinator within the global financial services ecosystem.

Apis Raises First Fund of USD 287 Million in 2015

When Matteo and Udayan launched the fundraising for their first fund, named Apis Growth Fund I, they were surprised by the support they received. One of their first commitments was from a friend of Stefanel's father, who decided to invest in Apis just five minutes into listening to them talk about it. Yet another meeting, this time with a high-net-worth individual based in New York, took four hours, because this particular investor wasn't immediately convinced of Apis' potential. Goyal and Stefanel were nothing if not persuasive and tenacious, and at the end of the meeting, they walked out having clinched a USD 15 million commitment! Both of them also reached out to Leapfrog's founders Andy Kuper and Jim Roth. Kuper founded Leapfrog in 2007, with the goal of synergizing profit and purpose. LeapFrog's methodology is to invest in exceptional businesses in Africa and Asia that deliver essential services to the emerging consumer. The firm partners with owners and leaders to achieve growth, profitability and impact, generating strong financial returns and changing millions of lives.

When Stefanel and Goyal reached out to Kuper and Roth, Leapfrog had raised USD 400 million for their second fund. The meeting went extremely well, and Roth and Kuper promptly introduced Stefanel and Goyal to all of their investors. Stefanel and Goyal were surprised by Kuper's kindness given that Apis could potentially become a competitor to LeapFrog in future: this was a true example of 'coopetition'! Fundraising was grueling but successful: after approaching 750 clients, Apis raised USD 287 million for Fund I, a phenomenal achievement for a first-time fund focused on Africa and South Asia. Matteo and Udayan's experience in financial services and fintech was one of the main reasons for this support.

Focus on Cashless to Drive Financial Inclusion

A key area that Apis has focused on and invested significantly in is reducing the cash involved in financial transactions by leveraging technology. Their view is that this is an important pillar for financial inclusion. One of the biggest challenges of financial inclusion is accessing the underserved or unserved customers who are often hard to reach, while making sure that the unit cost associated with reaching those customers is not high. This is especially difficult when these customers are in small towns and rural areas and the transaction sizes of these customers are small. The high fixed costs of traditional branch-based financial services distribution infrastructure mean that reaching these underserved segments on a commercially viable basis is difficult. For instance, if the cost associated with servicing a USD 1,00,000 loan is USD 100, it forms a small part of the overall cost of the loan. However, if the loan amount is only USD 1,000, then even if you reduce the cost to USD 50, it still amounts to 5 per cent of the loan and becomes prohibitively expensive. Microfinance has tried to address this by grouping customers together and handling them as a group rather than individually. However, there are limitations to this, since not every customer can be included in a group.

According to a study published in Harvard Business Review,[2] the attractiveness of cashless transactions is highest in cases where the cost of cash is high (convenience, transport, security), where technology uptake is accelerating, or where governments struggle to collect sales tax. Emerging economies exhibit all of these traits. That is why these economies, and their citizens, are often the prime beneficiaries of cashless transactions. The development of technology has facilitated the creation of newer and cheaper distribution mechanisms to reach populations that previously could not be reached. Not only has it improved the ability to reach these customers, but that access is now at a much lower cost, as the marginal cost of processing a digital transaction is zero.

While going cashless makes the lives of consumers and MSMEs easier and improves access and affordability, it also creates a significant macro level impact. According to research by BCG,[3] emerging economies can boost their annual GDP by over three percentage points by transitioning to a cashless economy—driven by faster value transfers, greater transparency and improved access to financing. Reducing cash also increases the capital available for investment in growth. It also helps central banks monitor the economy better. This helps to improve monetary and economic policy decisions and reduce illicit activities, such as money laundering and tax avoidance. The way Apis visualizes the impact from cashless transformation is shown in the table below:

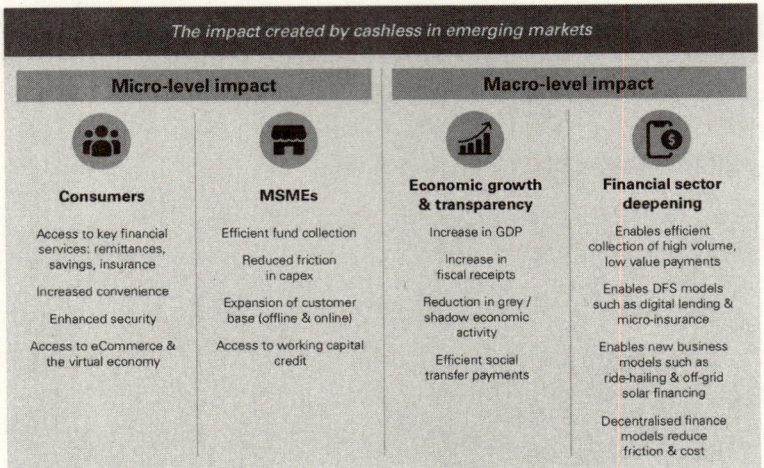

Figure 11: Impact created by cashless in emerging markets

*Source: 'The Importance of Cashless for Impact in Growth Markets',
Medium, https://medium.com/apis-insights/the-importance-of-cashless-for-
impact-in-growth-markets-5792c413a83a.*

In 2020, the global COVID-19 pandemic shut down the world, and provided a fresh momentum for cashless transactions and greater financial inclusion. The pandemic drove an increase in digital payments, amid a broader global expansion of formal financial services.[4] Stefanel and Goyal were early spotters of this trend that would develop through the pandemic. They had always believed that cashless transactions were an important criterion for driving financial inclusion in emerging markets. By 2020, Apis portfolio companies were processing 1.6 billion transactions amounting to USD 22.7 billion per annum. Apis considers the ability for consumers and MSMEs to make non-cash-based payments and to save funds electronically as the first step to improve access to formal financial services. As a result, Apis has focused extensively on investing in companies that are increasing non-cash payment transactions for retail and business customers. The view is that such 'electronification' of financial systems in emerging markets will give rise to additional digital financial services ('DFS'), including credit and insurance, built on top of this cashless transaction infrastructure.

Apis Growth Fund I Delivers Top Quartile Returns

Apis made ten investments from Apis Growth Fund I, focusing on driving inclusion across Asia and Africa by leveraging technology and expanding cashless penetration in line with their philosophy. As mentioned above, the fund has made significant difference in helping transform economies across several countries in Africa and Asia into cashless societies. It has already exited or announced the exit of nine of its ten investments. Direct Pay Online (DPO), one of those ten investments, is a great example of how enabling cashless payments across Africa has led to extensive transformation in the economy and in turn handsome returns for shareholders.

Democratizing Access to Financial Services in Africa While Delivering 50 Per Cent IRR[5]

In 2006, Kenyan Airlines approached Eran Feinstein, the co-founder of DPO, to help with technology to process online bookings and payments made by overseas visitors. While working on the project, Feinstein himself relocated to Kenya. Here, he began 3G Direct Pay in 2006. Within a decade, the business expanded to eight countries, serving 5800 merchants and by 2016, it was handling five million transactions with a total value of USD 600 million. But in order to scale up significantly, Feinstein knew that he would need an injection of capital. That was where Apis entered the picture.

When Stefanel and Goyal met Feinstein at the airport café in Nairobi in 2016, they saw right away that there was special potential here. They could see 3G Direct Pay helping to address the significant demand from merchants across Africa for affordable payment acceptance solutions. This would allow merchants to help the consumers pay online. This initial meeting was followed up with more detailed ones. Eventually, a deal took shape: Apis invested USD 10 million in 3G Direct Pay in 2016 and topped it up in follow-on rounds to USD 33.4 million. Given Apis' wide experience and its skilled team members, Apis pushed Feinstein to work towards acquiring companies, in order to build on areas like product, customer acquisitions and technology. Apis helped DPO identify specific merger and acquisitions (M&A) opportunities and assisted in structuring these transactions.

Immediately after investing, Apis worked closely with 3G Direct Pay, as the company went ahead to merge with Paygate. Apis also suggested renaming the business to Direct Pay Online (DPO). Over the next four years, DPO made four more acquisitions including Virtual Card Services, Paythru, PayFast and SiD Secure EFT, as they continued to expand their presence across geographies. Apis also helped DPO gain and retain key merchant accounts such as Mastercard, Uber and Jumia, resulting in strong organic growth[6] in the businesses. Today, the DPO Group is the leading payments service provider in Africa, with presence in fourteen countries across the continent. DPO serves tens of thousands of merchants in Africa, including leading e-commerce and travel and tourism-related businesses. The group accepts all major payment cards, mobile money and e-wallets, and is a leader in technology, usability and security. It introduced a revolutionary mobile application that enables merchants to process cards, contactless and Mobile Money payments.

Within five years of Apis' investment, DPO expanded its business to twenty-one countries, increasing the merchant base more than ten times to over 60,000 merchants, resulting in payment volumes growing 14x to 70 million transactions, worth nearly USD 3 billion. This led to several awards, including being listed among the CDC[7] Group's Impact Gamechangers 2021. However, the best recognition was in the form of acquisition by Network International for USD 291.3 million in 2021. This led to a return of 5.1x for Apis, implying an IRR of 50 per cent.

Metric	At Investment (2016)	At Exit (2021)
Countries	8	21
Merchants	5,800	60,000+
Revenue	USD 3 million	USD 37 million
Payment Volume	5 million	70 million
Payment Value	USD 600 million	USD 3 billion

Figure 12: Key metrics of DPO before Apis Investment and at Exit

There were several accomplishments beyond the financial returns. DPO enabled the deepening of financial services sector in Africa by improving the payments infrastructure. This was especially handy during COVID-19 as a significant number of transactions shifted online. The deal also resulted in a massive pay day for some of the DPO's employees. The employee stock option plan (ESOP) designed by Apis generated USD 11 million for over 400 DPO employees upon exit. In fact, some long-serving DPO janitorial staff received four times their annual salaries as part of this plan.

Apis Growth Fund II Is Also on Track to Deliver Top Quartile Performance

The great performance of Fund I helped Apis raise USD 563 million for Apis Growth Fund II, a 2019 vintage fund. Apis continued to focus on improving financial access for underserved across Asia and Africa. It made eleven investments from Fund II and has already achieved one exit and two partial exits to date, which is a remarkable achievement in such a short period of time. One of its success stories is MNT-Halan, which has had a massive impact on inclusion across Egypt.

MNT-Halan: Financial Super App Solving for Access to Finance, Payments and Savings

In 2007, while trying to figure out a topic for his undergraduate dissertation, Mounir Nakhla chose 'Impact of Microfinance in Egypt'. He chose it because his uncle was involved in the sustainable development space, and he thought he would be able to do some quality research. While conducting surveys for his dissertation, he realized the huge impact possible just by providing access to financial services for the unbanked and underbanked. In 2009, he founded MNT and started his journey in financial services by offering credit for purchasing Bajaj three-wheelers. Soon after, he obtained a microfinance license. He also started developing technology to improve access. In 2015, with the objective of exploring what was happening in the world of technology, he reached out and met people at technology companies such as Gojek, one of the largest ride-hailing services in south-east Asia. That visit opened his eyes to the potential of technology. During this visit, he met Ahmed Mohsen, who agreed to come onboard as co-founder, and partner with Mounir in his endeavour to leverage technology to improve access to financial services for the bottom of the pyramid in Egypt.

Given the expertise of his co-founder, Mounir also launched a ride-hailing service, Halan, in 2018, but decided to shut it down a couple of years later and focus on financial services, including developing a core banking software that was designed to offer customizable financial services. MNT and Halan merged in 2018, creating the MNT–Halan group, which also ventured into payments, offering a mobile wallet and card, since digital payments were an important part of financial inclusion. The mobile wallet scaled up rapidly. Today, they see services transactions of more than USD 100 million every month. Gradually, MNT added other financial products that encouraged savings including investments, gold and money market funds.

MNT evolved into the largest, fastest growing and most profitable non-bank lender in Egypt, driven by significant under-penetration of financial services in Egypt, where household debt/GDP is only 9 per cent, as compared to 70 per cent for many developed economies (as of 2022). Through its various subsidiaries, MNT was addressing this demand for credit. One of the subsidiaries named Tasaheel evolved into Egypt's large microfinance company, addressing the capital needs of unserved and underserved micro-enterprises both in urban and rural areas. Another subsidiary, Mashroey, became Egypt's leading asset backed lender while two other subsidiaries, Halan and Raseedy, facilitated transition towards digital payments and improved efficiencies across the board.

In 2021, Apis invested USD 47.6 million in MNT, as they saw a huge opportunity in driving digital financial inclusion in Egypt, especially as this is a country where less than 50 per cent of consumers have a bank account, yet mobile penetration exceeds 90 per cent. MNT's enablement of financial inclusion by addressing constraints that retail and MSME segments face in accessing formal credit helped to unlock the potential of an underdeveloped microfinance and retail credit sector in

Egypt. Apis helped MNT with the further digitization of its operations and broadening of its branch networks, which has resulted in the company now serving more than 2.3 million people quarterly, with 1.1 billion active borrowers.

As a result, MNT developed several structural advantages. The large distribution footprint across Egypt is hard for competitors to replicate, especially given MNT's superior technology which helps reduce the cost of distribution.

Apis continues to support Mounir Nakhla in his endeavour to expand MNT's reach to up to 15 million customers and grow beyond Egypt. In fact, Apis participated in a USD 160 million round raised by MNT in Jul 2024 with the objective of scaling up MNT across the region.

In addition to being top quartile performers, Apis' funds also make a substantial impact on the lives of low-and middle-income people in emerging markets. Apis' portfolio companies have served more than 180 million customers and 1.5 million SMEs directly. Going forward, Apis is expanding its horizon beyond emerging markets, but the impact thesis continues to remain similar—financial inclusion, financial literacy and financial wellness. Apis evaluates the impact of its potential investments and portfolio across three dimensions—Access, Quality and Markets.

Access: Provide essential financial services, products and infrastructure with a focus on low- and middle-income communities.

Quality: Such products and services should result in an improvement in quality of life (including higher income and savings) for customers and other stakeholders.

Markets: Generate high quality and equal opportunity employment.

Apis developed Apis Impact Management System (AIMS) , a proprietary tool, to measure, manage and report the impact of its portfolio. AIMS was created with the objective of providing specificity for measuring impact within financial services, through collection of quantitative as well as qualitative data that is arranged in mutually exclusive, collectively exhaustive (MECE) groupings. It incorporates the five dimensions of impact outlined by Impact Frontiers. It also reports on contributions to UN Sustainable Development Goals (SDGs) and incorporates ESG risk mitigation metrics.

Apis' Biggest Impact Is the Value It Adds to Its Portfolio Companies

Apis has consistently helped its portfolio companies to build value by leveraging its experience in financial services to help navigate individual challenges. With DPO, for instance, this took the form of helping the company increase its presence throughout the continent through acquisitions to help them find the right strategic partner. In MNT-Halan, Apis was heavily involved in digitizing operations and driving growth. In some cases, like that of Sun King (earlier known as Greenlight Planet), Apis has worked with management to redefine the business model to unlock significant value. Sun King is the world's leading off-grid solar energy company today. It designs, distributes, installs and finances solar energy solutions for those who cannot access or afford traditional electrical grid connections. The products offered range from cost-effective and durable solar powered lamps to energy systems that can power entire homes and businesses. Sun King has sold more than 100 million products to users across sixty-five countries in the world. Prior to Apis' investment in 2017, Greenlight Planet focused on selling the products directly. However, that meant that the customers who needed these products the most often could not afford to pay the full cost of the products. Apis worked with Sun King to develop a pay as you go solution, which meant that the consumer could pay as if they were paying for electricity rather than the equipment. This required careful consideration to understand how these payments fit with equipment costs and credit risk. It also required a mindset change to think like a lending business. Once this solution was implemented, Sun King's growth improved significantly. This, in turn, led to a USD 260 million investment led by General Atlantic's BeyondNetZero, helping them scale their solutions across Africa.

Apis' superior performance across both funds is driven by its ability to unlock massive productivity with the right financial tools. As Apis expands, both in size and geographical coverage, it continues to take us closer to the goal of achieving financial inclusion and financial wellness for unserved and underserved consumers globally.

8

Capria Ventures: Solving Critical Challenges Across the Global South

Dave Richards caught the software bug right from high school. It was the early 1980s, and the keyword in the world of technology was 'microprocessor'. This vital little chip—the home of a computer's most essential functions—had come into being many years earlier. But while Dave was growing up, it took on a life of its own. As he finished high school, it was an exciting time to be a tech geek. IBM launched the personal computer, which changed the game for computer technology. By the time Dave was in college, at the University of British Columbia in Vancouver, Canada, names that we recognize even today had hit the market. Bill Gates arrived on the tech scene with his Microsoft Windows. Right out of the gate, it was clear that Microsoft was going to be the kind of powerhouse that would rule the world of software for decades to come. As Dave himself admitted on the CEO Wisdom Podcast, he never looked back.[1] After all, there was no reason to. Computer technology was obviously changing the world, and in the 1980s, this was happening nearly every month. From the launch of the Apple Macintosh and Hewlett Packard's LaserJet printer to Nintendo's entertainment system for the video game industry. Dave was majoring in business and finance, but he was so hooked to the countless innovations he saw in computer technology that he spent nearly every spare moment holed up in the computer lab on campus, writing code and building his own software skills.

He knew that for him, a career path lay in software. Dave's first few years of his career as a tech professional were at software companies in Vancouver, Canada, before he took the decision to move to Silicon Valley, where he began working in a management position at the tech giant, Symantec. In the late 1980s, Symantec was in the process of transitioning into being a major supplier of security software. Dave worked there and at Sybase for a total of eight years, developing breakthrough technologies, including infrastructure for the emerging Internet.

From Silicon Valley, Dave decided to shift to Seattle, another tech hub and the home of companies such as Microsoft and Amazon, to join RealNetworks. Originally known as Progressive Networks, RealNetworks was founded in 1994 by former Microsoft executive Rob Glaser. Initially aimed at distributing politically progressive content, it soon evolved into a technology venture leveraging the Internet as an alternative medium for audio broadcasts. RealNetworks became the pioneer of the streaming media market when it broadcast an audio event—a baseball game between the New York Yankees and the Seattle Mariners—on 5 September 1995. The success of this was so instant that barely two years later, RealNetworks announced streaming video technology, and began trading on NASDAQ in 1997.

After eight years at RealNetworks, Dave moved out and co-founded two tech start-ups—one in the digital media space and another as a marketplace that matched home trade-contractors with homeowners for the purpose of maintenance and renovations. In the end, one of these companies merged with another and the other needed to be shut down. He also helped multiple other new enterprises get off the ground. In the process, he learned a lot about start-ups, but more importantly, he developed the conviction that technology could have a significant impact on people's lives.

At the dawn of the new millennium, Dave got introduced to microcredit, which was, at the time, attracting global attention. Microcredit, also known as microfinance, is part of a wider category of financial services that target individuals and very small businesses. In simple terms, microcredit is the extension of very small loans (microloans) to low-income borrowers, who typically lack collateral, steady employment or even a verifiable credit history. As a concept, it is designed to support entrepreneurship and increase their earning power. As discussed in the first part of this book, microfinance was popularized by the success of Grameen Bank that Mohammad Yunus founded in Bangladesh in 1983. Dave's introduction to this fascinating new world came through his father, who was then on the board of World Vision, the second largest non-governmental organization in the United States after the Red Cross. At the time, World Vision was evaluating microcredit as a potential way to help low-income people in emerging countries become self-reliant through micro-business self-employment.[2]

It was at this point that Dave got connected to Unitus, which had attracted a group of successful entrepreneurs who came together with the objective of leveraging their skills, resources and network for social good. The team at Unitus visited Muhammad Yunus, the founder of the microcredit pioneer Grameen Bank, and spent couple of weeks in Bangladesh studying its microfinance model. At the end of the meeting with Yunus,[3] the group posed a question to him 'If we had USD 100 million, what would you recommend we do?' Yunus' response was brief but clear. He said, 'Replicate what I've done here in other developing countries.' From there on, the growth of microfinance became the mission for Unitus. It evolved into a catalytic organization that backed about twenty-five different start-up microfinance institutions across various countries, including India, south-east Asia, Africa and Latin America. It helped these institutions get off the ground by providing access to the best practices, assisting in raising debt and grant capital initially, and eventually helping them secure equity as they scaled up.

Dave ended up getting involved just at the stage where Unitus was starting to pick the entrepreneurs they wanted to back. He was a board member at that point and had decided India was going to be the most interesting of all the countries in which Unitus was present. He signed up to be the India lead in the mid-2000s. This offered him a great opportunity to visit rural areas where various fledgling microfinance organizations were operating. Many of these organizations are household names today—SKS (now Bharat Financial Inclusion), Equitas, Bandhan and Ujjivan. And over time, they evolved into some of the most well-known microfinance companies and later became banks serving lower-income communities.

Unitus helped these organizations raise the first round of capital that would go into building strong foundations. As a first step, even before helping them to raise equity, Unitus helped them to raise debt so that these companies could extend loans to their customers. Effectively, the company became an investment bank, as it helped these organizations raise tens of millions of dollars in debt and equity. Ultimately, the investment banking business was spun out separately as Unitus Capital. Today, it is one of the most active investment banks in India, especially in raising capital for financial services companies. Unitus also set up one of the first private capital venture funds for microfinance called the Unitus Equity Fund, which was spun out as Elevar Equity. In addition, in 2011, Unitus also incubated and launched Patamar Capital, an impact venture capital firm investing in South-east Asian markets.

In India, Dave was asked to lead projects focused on innovations beyond microfinance. During the process, he was approached by many entrepreneurs who were innovating in areas such as agriculture, healthcare and mobility, and were looking for seed capital. Dave felt that there was a huge opportunity and spoke with a few of his partners, including Will Poole, a senior executive at Microsoft who led the Windows business globally. He also spoke to Srikrishna Ramamoorthy, who was on the investment team at the Michael & Susan Dell Foundation and on the founding team of Ujjivan, a microfinance pioneer, about launching an early-stage venture capital seed fund in India.

They were all convinced on the opportunity and began to raise money from outside India, as well as from prominent individuals within the country, including Mohandas Pai (ex-CFO of Infosys), Ranjan Pai (Chairman of Manipal group) and Hemendra Kothari (DSP Blackrock). These influential, wealthy families provided not only financial capital but also crucial access to credible and powerful networks—an invaluable asset for a start-up seed fund in India.

Birth of Capria Ventures

In 2013, Dave and his partners launched one of the first private capital seed fund in India and named it Unitus Seed Fund (India Fund I), managed by Unitus Ventures (later renamed to Capria Ventures). The fund was focused on the next half a billion people in India (outside of the top 100 million people) that the partners defined as the aspiring middle class. Simply put, these were the lower and lower-middle classes who aspired for more in their lives. India Fund I backed entrepreneurs serving these large groups of underserved people in a profitable and scalable way. It focused on sectors such as healthcare, education, agriculture, mobility and new models of e-commerce, which reached out beyond the big cities.

Dave and his partners believed that there would eventually be large businesses focused on the aspiring middle class. In many ways, it was a pioneering model. There weren't many entrepreneurs who worked or focused on that space. Existing venture capital firms were primarily backing 'avocado start-ups'[4]—those serving the higher income segments in the big metros. Almost all the entrepreneurs they encountered at this point were first timers, albeit with a wide variety of experiences which mostly didn't include working in a start-up. Right from the beginning, Dave and his partners focused on transparency and accountability. From the start, they told their investors that they would be screening for companies that delivered impact to the aspiring middle class. They committed to report annually on the progress that was being made on this front. They were one of the first funds to start presenting and creating not only a screening process and system for tracking generated impact, but also to report on the tracking mechanisms. In 2014, they published their first annual impact report[5] in which they shared their impact measurement framework and reported that their portfolio companies touched 46,756 lives at the Bottom of the Economic Pyramid (BoP)[6] and created 267 jobs.

Impact screening was a critical part of the investment process. The focus was on improving lives and livelihoods and/or access to affordable and accessible products and services through investing in job-tech, financial inclusion, healthcare, food and agriculture and more. They were looking for sustainable businesses that, while serving the consumers at low-price points, had the ability to deliver profitability on a per customer basis.

Attractive unit economics[7] that could lead to profitable and sustainable business was a critical parameter for evaluating these opportunities. According to Dave, one of the things that they learnt very early on is that if they weren't investing in businesses that had sound business models, these companies were not going to be able to raise further capital to realize their potential. They were trying to find businesses that had compelling unit economics. As they were a seed fund with limited capital 'bridge funding' them to prove that they were ready to scale up, these businesses needed next stage growth investors who were more risk adverse. Great business models with impact inherently built-in will, as they scale up, also scale up their impact. If the business has poor unit economics, then it's not going to scale, and the impact isn't going to scale. Dave believes that it is in their DNA that they care so much about impact being realized at scale that they need to make sure they invested in great businesses!

Capria's India Fund I Is on Track to Be a Top Quartile Fund

Capria's first India fund made twenty-three investments across sectors, including agriculture, healthcare, education, mobility and business services. It is on track to be a top quartile fund among all the funds raised in 2013, thanks to performance of companies like Betterplace, which is likely to return the whole fund.

Betterplace Addresses the Needs of Frontline Workers

Betterplace was founded by Pravin Agarwala and Saurabh Tandon in 2015. Pravin was worried about the safety of his daughters and other children after he heard about a mishap in the neighbourhood school that was caused by an employee's inefficient verification process. This inspired him to start Betterplace which, at the time, was a platform that could affordably verify the people enterprises hired so that they could ensure a safe working environment.

Through the years, Pravin started noticing that verification was just one of the many issues plaguing the Indian frontline workforce space. There were also other issues, such as access and living conditions. BetterPlace started revolutionizing workforce management by tackling critical issues in the hiring process. Its digital solution streamlines sourcing and onboarding, eliminating the need for physical or manual intervention. Addressing the productivity challenge, BetterPlace introduced a bot-based mobile app for upskilling employees based on their needs, spanning from language proficiency to financial literacy. The auto-rostering system fulfils time and attendance requirements, ensuring efficiency. Moreover, BetterPlace automates salary calculations and disbursement. Beyond this, the platform leverages recorded work and financial data to offer users access to benefits like insurance and credit, providing a comprehensive solution for workforce empowerment.

Today, BetterPlace is Asia's largest workforce management SaaS platform, delivering digital solutions for enterprises to manage the entire lifecycle of their frontline workers. It enables millions in the blue-collar workforce to access jobs, skills and training in their local language, as well as banking solutions, credit, insurance, quality healthcare and more—by providing solutions that build and leverage their digital profiles.

Since 2015, BetterPlace has transformed over 1500 businesses while serving 500 locations across the APAC, India and GCC regions. It oversees USD 1.5 billion in employee payroll, facilitating over 300 million minutes of training and seamlessly handling background verifications for over twenty-six million individuals through their cutting-edge platform.

BetterPlace has acquired and integrated four companies during 2023 and 2024, enhancing its skilling, staffing, workflow building and short-term gig staffing capabilities. These include

Oust Labs (skilling), Aasaan Jobs (staffing), Ezedox (no-code workflow builder), OkayGo (short-term gig staffing platform) and Bueno Finance (fintech offering credit and earned wage access to gig workers).

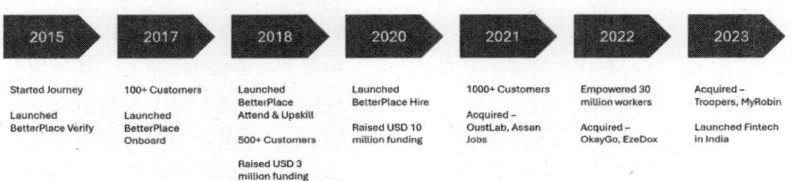

Figure 13 : Evolution of BetterPlace

Source: 'About Us', BetterPlace Global, [May 2024],
https://www.betterplaceglobal.com/about-us

BetterPlace addressed two significant pain points for the frontline workforce in India—the informal nature of work and low income. More than 90 per cent of India's workforce works in the informal sector. This means they do not have access to social security, making them vulnerable to external shocks. Additionally, because this workforce is not formalized, they do not have minimum wage guarantees or access to skills that can help them enhance their earning potential. Hence, their salaries have remained stagnant in real terms. BetterPlace has formalized more than 30 million workers through its platform, accounting for 10 per cent of the overall frontline workforce in India. By doing so, it has increased workers' earning potential by 50 per cent by providing them with access to skilling courses and gig work.

Capria Ventures was the first institutional investor in BetterPlace investing USD 3,00,000 in its 2016 seed round when its potential was a 'glimmer in the eye' of the founding team. Capria's team saw the potential for the huge shift from the informal to the formal economy in India that had the opportunity to positively impact tens of millions of people. They saw that BetterPlace, with its technology and approach, had the potential to enable people at the bottom and middle of the economic pyramid to move up and become a part of the formal economy. Fueled by technology, BetterPlace's platform acts as a bridge, addressing the efficiency and productivity challenges enterprises face and the aspirations of individual frontline workers. In Dave's words, 'India's demographic dividend with 10 million youth turning 18 years old per year, rising digital adoption with 850 million internet subscribers, conducive public policy, and a thriving gig economy with 7 million gig workers make BetterPlace a catalyst for India's USD 5 trillion economy dream.'

Since then, as the company has demonstrated progress, it has raised more capital from investors, including VH Capital, 3one4 Capital, Jungle Ventures, British International Investment (UK government development fund) and Macquarie Capital in additional funding rounds, along with Capria investing more. As of December 2023, BetterPlace has raised more than USD 80 million in equity financing. Capria plans to sell its stake in the not-too-distant future, which will not only generate a profit on this one investment but could also return to its investors the entire capital invested in India Fund I—potentially up to 2x the entire fund investment (invested across twenty-three companies) or even more. This reflects the VC investing strategy of outlier successful investments in a few companies for each fund where the 'winners pay for the losers'. Many of the investments in the fund will be write-offs returning no capital—the start-up tried to disrupt the market but ultimately failed, and they lost their investment. A highly successful investment like BetterPlace enables them to still deliver an attractive return to their fund investors.

Capria Ventures Expands to Other Emerging Markets After Success in India

In 2016, Capria Ventures launched an initial pilot fund to expand beyond India into some of the other top tech hubs of the Global South. For this new Global South Fund I, Capria aimed to focus on early growth-stage investments—slightly later than the seed-stage investments they had been making in India. In order to get access to the best deals in each tech hub city and to be able to support those deals through their different stages of growth, they wanted to have early-stage local venture capital firms in each of the markets they were investing in. So, they set up their first Global South Fund as a 'fund of funds'—investing in local VC Funds and then making co-investments with those partner funds.

Capria made commitments to fifteen local VC Funds. They chose not just the regions, but also the cities, where they thought a lot of tech innovation was happening. After India (with Bangalore as its primary hub), they expanded into Latin America backing funds based in Sao Paulo, Mexico City and some up-and-coming places, such as Santiago and Buenos Aires. They then expanded into Africa, focusing on Lagos and Nairobi plus up-and-coming North Africa and GCC tech hub, Cairo. And then they added south-east Asia, where they focused on Jakarta and Ho Chi Minh City along with Singapore as a regional hub.

While investing in funds, Capria focused on local fund managers who were intentional about the impact that they want to create. For instance, they invested in a Brazilian fund that focused on the agri and food tech space with the intention of driving the sustainability of farming by helping farmers cope with climate change and improving the livelihood of farmers. Another fund is focused on financial inclusion in south-east Asia. They focus on an overall portfolio impact target and require funds to report the impact of their portfolio annually to Capria. One of the critical characteristics they were looking for in the fund managers was the willingness to learn and to be collaborative. They have helped a lot of them by providing toolkits to develop their impact and ESG frameworks and integrate impact into their screening and reporting processes.

In 2018, Capria Ventures launched its second India seed fund (India Fund II), which is already trending to be a top-quartile fund performer. It invested in sixteen companies across sectors including job-tech, health and education. While India Fund II also invested in some successes in India Fund I, such as BetterPlace, it also has potential fund returners such as Eduvanz, an education financing company.

Eduvanz: Financing Education at Every Level

Founded in 2016 by Varun Chopra and Raheel Shah, Eduvanz is one of India's leading student loan providers. Varun discovered that many parents and students lacked financial support when they earlier had set up CurrEQlum, a dedicated platform to nurture children's skills, with a focus on enhancing children's emotional intelligence (EQ). This revelation led to launching Eduvanz with the vision to build a gateway to accessible education by addressing the financial barriers.

Eduvanz is a non-banking financial institution that provides education loans at zero percent interest. It revolutionizes education financing, prioritizing faster loan decisions, transparency and student-centric policies. By customizing loan solutions for all stakeholders, learners benefit from fast, affordable and flexible financial support, increasing enrolments for education institutions with expedited disbursals. Integrated seamlessly with technology platforms of educational institutes, Eduvanz offers a streamlined loan journey, making upfront fee payments based on agreed loan products. With a focus on zero-cost loan solutions for up to twenty-four months, Eduvanz ensures parents and learners can repay conveniently through affordable equal monthly installment (EMI) payments. The entirely online, paperless process, coupled with proprietary AI algorithms, enables a swift and future-focused loan journey.

Education financing incumbents are largely focused on the large-ticket higher education loan segment. Financing for upskilling (to get a better paying job), K-12 and test prep courses are underserved. Eduvanz is filling a critical financing gap and directly addressing aspiring middle-class needs, as 45% of Eduvanz loans are to students from lower-income families (with a monthly household income of less than USD 500), and 64 per cent of Eduvanz's borrowers come from tier 2 and 3 cities. Furthermore, 21 per cent of borrowers are taking a formal loan for the first time, and in the process, they are taking their first step to building a reliable credit history. There isn't much formal competition as most lenders focus on financing overseas education, and most students, who are not looking for overseas education, revert to informal networks. Banks (and other loan agencies) in India are nervous about the collections from education-related loans, so they are reluctant to offer these loans or only offer them at high-interest rates. Vocational lending is an extensive USD 5 billion white space that Eduvanz is well positioned to lead.

With the ongoing changes to work requirements, workers today are required to skill, upskill and reskill themselves regularly. This continuous need for learning has resulted in great demand for relevant educational courses and an infrastructure that can support this change digitally. Today, more than ever, India is the youngest it has ever been, with over 140 million young Indians aged 18–25 who will need meaningful employment and skills. Prior to Eduvanz, there wasn't a scaled player serving Indian students/workers with financing for India-based education, especially in programmes that are directly focused on less-than-one-year courses directly connected to an upgraded job. Eduvanz has built financial products supported by innovative loan policies that resonate with the Indian learning ecosystem— thereby building win-win outcomes for all the stakeholders. Up to December 2023, the company has financially empowered over 1,85,000 learners across twenty Indian states (240 cities) and covered over twenty-five skill industries through partnerships with 900 institutes and thirteen lending partners.

Capria Ventures was the first institutional investor in Eduvanz investing USD 5,00,000 in 2018 for its seed financing round from its India Fund II. Since then, Peak XV Partners (formerly Sequoia India), Juvo Capital and RTE Ventures also invested in subsequent financing rounds, along with Capria investing more. As of December 2023, Eduvanz has raised USD 29 million in equity and multiples of that amount in debt financing. While it's still too early to know what level of investment return Capria will be able to realize here, if Eduvanz can continue to execute well, there is a reasonable probability that Capria will be able to return all the capital investors put in from the returns of its investment in Eduvanz India Fund II creating a 'fund returner' outcome.

Strong Performance Has Enabled Capria to Raise New Funds

In early 2023, Capria launched both an India Opportunity Fund to invest in the growth stages of the break-out companies from India funds as well as its second Global South Fund structured as an early-stage venture fund. In September 2023, they decided to consolidate their branding under 'Capria', dropping the Unitus branding to simplify messaging. They have the same ownership and common global back office and shared services support including portfolio value creation, marketing, operations and finance with distributed diverse team based in Seattle, Bangalore, Nairobi, Jakarta, Mexico City, Washington DC and Buenos Aires.

A Concentrated Portfolio Compared to Other Seed Funds

Capria has purposefully kept to a more concentrated portfolio compared to other seed funds, enabling them to dedicate more support to each founding team. A lot of seed funds of their size would invest in thirty or forty companies; however, Capria's seed funds I and II have invested in twenty-three and sixteen companies, respectively. They have invested around 60 per cent in initial investments, and reserve 40 per cent to invest in the best companies for at least one or two follow-on rounds.

Focus on Strategy and Execution to Support Portfolio

Capria has made more than sixty investments in eleven years, of which about thirty-five are currently active. This puts massive pressure on the team for portfolio management. For their seed investments, the approach is to be very actively involved in the first couple of years until they bring in another lead investor for a follow-on round. They can then gradually reduce their day-to-day involvement and focus on coaching and supporting the founders while continuing to be a major voice at the board level. In most cases, the new investors want them to be involved because they have the history. When they initially invest at the early-growth stage, they partner with co-investors and focus more on what they can uniquely bring to the table from a value-add perspective.

The typical areas they add value to for early-stage companies are refining core business strategy and supporting execution. As operators, they have empathy for entrepreneurs and understand the challenges of operating. They also help their companies with global connections, not just on the fundraising, but also to bring in expertise. They found that the founders of their companies are much more interested in talking to other founders than they are in talking to experts. So, they organize meetings for founders on various topics of interest, such as embedded finance and cost management. A lot of their companies operate in a similar space across markets. So, they also get to share learnings from different markets.

Leveraging Generative AI (GenAI) for Impact

The world was surprised in November 2022 with OpenAI's launch of ChatGPT, the first access most people had to a new generation of artificial intelligence. Then in the first half of 2023, the launch of APIs (application programming interfaces) from OpenAI and others along with the release of open source LLMs (large language models) was an even bigger gamechanger. These LLMs enabled human-like interaction with computers and also helped with text-to-picture and text-to-video conversions. The models which enabled these were together labelled generative models and this subset of artificial intelligence was called Generative Artificial Intelligence or GenAI for short. Many tech start-ups 'born before' these events are at risk of becoming irrelevant and getting disrupted themselves by new start-ups that were conceived as 'GenAI first'. We all saw this happen when smartphones first launched and mobile-first start-ups often replaced incumbents that were desktop-first. According to Dave, GenAI is expected to have a 100x faster and wider impact than mobile phones, as it requires no additional hardware or infrastructure for adoption.

From the beginning, Capria saw a once-in-a-generation opportunity to accelerate impact through GenAI technology. They see GenAI as the 'great equalizer' enabling less educated people and non-English speakers to have access to the whole of the world's knowledge and to be an amplifier of their capabilities. It also has the possibility of helping many young people learn and leverage GenAI as 'natives' unlocking the demographic dividend of youthful populations. For tech-enabled start-ups, it can significantly lower product and service price points. This, coupled with ability and willingness to pay, can expand market opportunities by 2x, 5x or even 10x—reaching larger populations that would have been unsustainable without GenAI. This helps further scale the impact that Capria can deliver through its investments.

In December 2022, Capria made a strategic decision to bet on the application of GenAI for tech-enabled services businesses. Capria realized that the GenAI infrastructure (AI models) and tools were going to require billions of dollars of investment dominated by tech companies in the US and China with big Silicon Valley and China VC Funds fighting it out with a few big winners and lots of money lost on the rest. So, Capria chose to steer clear of those types of GenAI investments and instead focus on 'applied GenAI'—leveraging existing GenAI models to enhance the products and services of their portfolio companies rather than building the models themselves. For instance, one of the easy wins with GenAI is improving customer care experience and cost associated with that. The applications of GenAI are also where Capria expects most of the value (and money) to be created as entrepreneurs take these new capabilities and build a new generation of businesses in every industry.

Capria chose to support its existing portfolio to catch-up in implementing GenAI as both defence (against competitors adopting GenAI) and offence (to build next generation services with GenAI to expand their businesses). Capria started by developing thought leadership articles explaining how

GenAI was going to change operating businesses and sharing with portfolio company founders and its local investing partners. They also started hosting online round tables with portfolio CEOs, CTOs and other leaders to help them get support with this extremely fast-moving space. What they quickly discovered was that very few of the portfolio companies were equipped to make rapid progress with adopting GenAI.

In June 2023, Capria hired its first in-house GenAI developer with the goal of helping Capria to start building its own internal GenAI tools and to help portfolio companies to develop their initial GenAI prototypes. Within weeks, Capria launched a test version of its first internal tool, GUS—short for Get Us Smarter—which allowed team members to use conversational queries to answer common internal questions. A few months later, they launched 'IC Co-Pilot', which functioned as a co-pilot for the Capria investment team in building analysis reports for the investment committee, leveraging the firm's eleven years of evaluating investments.

Over the next few months, Capria helped multiple portfolio companies set up their first GenAI prototypes and then handed over to them for roll out. These included using GenAI to (a) improve the quality of customer support 24x7 while reducing the cost of customer support; (b) improving the functionality of the user experience for children learning math by personalizing in a way that was previously impossible; (c) creating a co-pilot for an outsource customer service company which 'listened' in on a call and provided instant resources for the customer service rep; and many more. In fact, the results were so profound that Capria decided in Q4 2023 to hire three additional full-time GenAI developers to expand their portfolio support.

Strong Performance Backed By Exits

With Capria's first two India seed funds tracking towards top quartile performance, and a promising start to its initial Global South Fund, its thesis of investing in great teams and businesses with built-in scaled impact seems to be delivering on both returns and impact. The Global South Fund, which invested about two-thirds of its capital in multiple local VC Funds, is intentionally expected to offer a slightly lower MOIC[8] (along with less downside) return because it is much more diversified (over 300 company investments). Dave notes that this performance has been driven by a combination of early exits and patience as their investments have taken time to grow in scale. One of their early investments is expected to return two to three times the size of the fund, i.e. the entire capital contributed by their investors in the fund (not just the investment in that company alone).

When to exit is a critical challenge of being an early-stage and early-growth investor. According to Dave, 'Part of the challenge when you're a seed investor is that there is this often a value increase power curve at the Series B or Series C funding rounds.' For instance, they had a situation where a company raised money at a USD 100 million valuation, and within a year, it already had offers at a USD 400 million valuation. And so, Dave feels that for early-stage funds timing an exit is a tricky question that requires balancing potential return and risk. Capria primarily expects to exit its investments through secondary sales to other investors and sometimes through trade deals with a small possibility (controlled by the markets) for an IPO. And, one of the things about a seed portfolio is that there is a serious power law. Unlike in private equity, where you have very few failures, seed investors expect 50-60 per cent of their investments to fail. So, the best companies must do really well to drive overall returns.

9

Future Planet Capital: Scaling
Innovation for People and Planet

After celebrating his fortieth birthday, Douglas Hansen-Luke, founder of Future Planet Capital, felt a growing desire to make a meaningful difference in society. Having built a successful career leading several asset management firms, including ABN Amro and Robeco, Douglas had achieved financial security and was ready to focus on a mission that could create a lasting impact. His journey towards this goal was a natural one.

A graduate in philosophy, politics and economics from the University of Oxford—where he ran the university newspaper, *Cherwell*—he knew early on that his strengths lay in strategy and communication. After beginning his career as a consultant with Bain, Douglas transitioned into the world of finance with Salomon Brothers in 1994, where he specialized in emerging market equities. Salomon Brothers, which was later acquired by Citibank, was one of the five largest investment banking enterprises in the United States, and an extremely profitable firm on Wall Street in 1980s and 1990s. As one of the leading underwriters of corporate bonds, and one of the top firms in futures and options, Salomon Brothers Inc. served many of the largest corporations in America.[1] It was at Salomon Brothers that he first recognized his passion for innovation. 'When I looked at emerging market equities, what I loved about it was a very clear sense of purpose.' He was excited about attracting capital to emerging markets, which helped in driving growth and uplifting people while delivering strong returns for investors.[2]

At Salomon Brothers, Douglas developed his quant skills, using derivatives to build index replication strategies that attracted significant investment into emerging markets. In turn, these created large orders for him as an equity sales professional. His early work laid the foundation for his later achievements. He co-founded a research firm backed by investors such as Hong Kong Telecom and Jardine Fleming (which was later acquired by JP Morgan) which combined technical analysis and quant research with fundamental analysis, to identify companies that were trading outside their usual bands. It did very well in a short period of time, helping investors achieve impressive returns. But these were the years of the notorious 'dot-com' bubble—also known as the tech boom, or the Internet bubble. It was a handful of years, really—from 1995 to 2001—but it changed the landscape of the technology sector and stock markets the world over. Essentially speaking, the influx of money into the web sector, coupled with the internet's explosive popularity, led to a dangerously rapid expansion in valuations. This was despite the fact that many of these new tech companies lacked concrete paths to profitability. In addition, low interest rates in the late 1990s made debt financing easier for young, ambitious tech companies to acquire, further fuelling the Internet industry's unchecked growth. In late 2000, these streams of easy money dried up, and the industry imploded, causing many tech companies to go under and ushering in a new bear market that would last for around two years and affect the entire stock market—not just the technology sector.

It was a whole new world for investors, and as a result, Hansen–Luke could not find enough funding support to keep the firm going. He moved into asset management with ABN Amro, where his innovative work continued. There, he had the opportunity to continue innovating with new asset classes, including the first hedge fund of funds for Asia, some of the first private equity funds, products for agri and real estate, the first China funds and the first Indian funds. He also worked on other innovative structured products, such as guaranteed return hedge funds and enhanced index funds.[3] It was work that was like the index replication that he had done for Salomon Brothers, but it was, in many ways, better. However, until today, the contribution that he is most proud of, during his time at ABN-Amro, was his involvement in responsible investing.[4] Responsible investment involves considering environmental, social and governance (ESG) issues when making investment decisions. It complements traditional financial analysis and portfolio construction techniques. Responsible investors can have different objectives. Some focus exclusively on financial returns and consider ESG issues that could impact these. Others aim to generate financial returns and to achieve positive outcomes for people and the planet, while avoiding negative ones.[5] In 2019, ABN Amro signed the UN Principles for Responsible Banking, together with 129 other international banks. The signatories, representing one-third of the total assets of all banks worldwide, agreed that they would align their business strategies with the United Nations Sustainable Development Goals and with the Paris Climate Agreement. The six principles for Responsible Investment offer a menu of possible actions for incorporating ESG issues into investment practice. With the focus being on their sustainable implementation, signatories (like ABN AMRO) would be helping to build and maintain a more equitable, sustainable financial system across the world.

For Hansen-Luke, this was just the first step in making a difference in the way investments were made. 'Understanding ESGs was something that was key to my work in 2003 to 2005,' he says, adding, 'I just found ESGs the easiest thing in the world to get my head around.' For Hansen-Luke, thinking of investments through the lens of ESG went without saying. According to him, ESG is additional information, and investors should consider all the information available to make their decisions. 'The second part about ESG is that you use that information to tell you truly what the risk adjusted return is,' he explains, adding, 'ESG is not really a moral decision. It's an intellectual decision.'[6]

In 2007, he followed one of the board members at ABN Amro to Robeco. Originally a Dutch asset management firm, Robeco was founded in 1929 as the **Ro**tterdamsch **Be**leggings **Co**nsortium (Rotterdam Investment Consortium or Robeco). As of 2014, the company had Euro246 billion worth of assets under its management.[7] Hansen-Luke joined as the CEO of Robeco (Middle East, Africa and Central Asia). At Robeco, there was a huge focus on sustainability as investor preferences, government regulations and even risks continued to change. The focus on climate change, social inequalities and the UN SDGs became fresh sources of innovation and growth for Robeco. In this context, the company had embarked on addressing challenges, such as climate change and water scarcity, way back in 2007. Robeco used a basic data-driven approach to address sustainability aspects. The glitch for Hansen-Luke was that collecting this kind of data, across different markets and listed equities, meant thirty-page long questionnaires. In Hansen-Luke's perspective, this wasn't a sustainable approach. 'I really liked the quant basis of it,' he says, adding, 'But I was sceptical of the long questionnaire element'. This insight pushed him towards his next venture.

In 2012, Douglas founded HLD Partners with a clear mission: to drive sustainable impact through emerging asset classes. HLD Partners advised large institutional investors and sovereign wealth funds, helping them define mandates and identify the right asset managers for their goals, whether focused on women's empowerment or sustainability. Hansen-Luke was very clear that he wanted to leverage quant to the maximum extent possible. Sustainable was the key word for him, and in his mind, it was inherently linked to profitability. This had been at the back of his mind since he had started his career, and now, his experience had taught him that the two could be—and were—intrinsically linked. Indeed, he believed that there was nothing sustainable about a venture that must close down and fire all its staff.

HLD Partners began advising large institutional investors and sovereign wealth funds, with a focus on impact and emerging asset classes. They would help these investors define a mandate and then help identify the right asset managers to fulfil that mandate. For instance, if the identified mandate was to invest with a focus on women empowerment, HLD Partners would identify how to go about it. This included helping clients to identify the right products and asset managers to address their specific needs. One of the challenges that they found difficult to address was the access to innovation at scale. Most of their clients could only invest in companies after they had matured, missing out on exposure to innovation that often delivers outsized returns.

This was a critical problem. Out of the top ten companies in the world today by market capitalization, six are technology driven and, in fact, the top five companies—Apple, Microsoft, Nvidia, Alphabet and Amazon—are all technology companies. Without access to innovation at early stages, clients would miss out on the opportunity to make strong returns. Interestingly, however, a lot of these companies that went on to become big names in their fields were actually products of innovation, born in the top universities. Google is a prime example. HLD Partners wanted to create a path for their clients to access this innovation but could not find the right asset managers to create that path.

This led Hansen-Luke to launch Future Planet Capital in 2015, with the goal of bridging the divide between institutional investors and the world's leading universities and research ecosystems. Today, Future Planet Capital has funded 140 companies across geographies and stages, addressing critical global challenges like climate change, education, health, security and sustainable growth—delivering both financial returns and positive societal impact. The firm now manages over USD 460 million, continuing its mission to invest in innovation that shapes a better future. Some of their portfolio companies innovating across different themes are shown below:

Theme	Portfolio Company	Description
Climate Change and Energy Security	Tokamak Energy	Tokamak Energy is revolutionizing the world's energy supply, aiming to develop commercial fusion energy in the next decade. In harnessing fusion, the same process that powers stars, Tokamak Energy could provide abundant, carbon-free power without harming the planet, contributing significantly to critical clean energy goals.
	Oxford Flow	Oxford Flow produces cutting-edge industrial pressure regulators that are enhancing performance across natural gas, water and industrial processes. Their stem-free valves combat fugitive methane leaks, a gas twenty-eight times more potent than CO_2, potentially preventing the release of 3.6 trillion cubic feet annually.
	Captura	Captura offers an innovative climate change solution by harnessing the ocean, the world's largest carbon removal device. Oceans naturally absorb 30 per cent of global CO_2 emissions. Powered by seawater and renewable electricity, Captura's systems enable the ocean to draw down additional CO_2 without raising oceanic levels. Seawater is drawn in, CO_2 extracted and securely stored or utilized for sustainable products. The process ensures net CO_2 removal without harming the ocean or requiring additional resources.
	Queen of Raw	Excess inventory has long plagued industries, leading to warehouse congestion and environmental harm when discarded in landfills and incinerators. Queen of Raw addresses this with their Materia MX software, streamlining global excess inventory management and facilitating reselling and recycling processes while enhancing workflow and financial reporting.

Sustainable and Resilience Supply Chains	Twig	Twig creates sustainable and environmentally friendly ingredients using a bio-based manufacturing platform. Taking chemicals away from oil-based manufacture and reducing reliance on farming for feedstocks, Twig frees up resources that could be used for food production or returned to nature. With growing populations and consumption patterns wreaking havoc on the environment, engineering biology offers sustainable solutions. Reprogramming microbes allows production of everyday ingredients from food industry waste, reducing reliance on fossil fuels and intensive farming. This approach promotes supply chain security, requiring only renewable energy and water.
	Solasta Bio	Traditional pesticides have very harmful environmental impacts, killing pollinators, contaminating water and disrupting ecosystems. Solasta Bio offers a nature-inspired solution with neuropeptide-based insecticides that are highly targeted against the crop pest sparing beneficial organisms and ecosystems. Moreover, Solasta's products reduce greenhouse gas emissions due to their highly efficient manufacture.
	Roslin Technologies	Roslin Technologies leads in supplying cell lines for cultivated protein, revolutionizing food production. Cultivated protein offers a sustainable solution, reducing carbon footprint, land usage and water consumption by over 90 per cent. Roslin's high-quality cell lines are crucial for safe, affordable and nutritious cultivated meat and seafood, driving a paradigm shift in agriculture and aquaculture.
	Tropic	Tropic Biosciences employs advanced gene editing, like CRISPR, to enhance crop resilience, nutrition and disease resistance, offering sustainable solutions for modern agriculture. Unlike conventional GMOs, their method targets precise genetic changes within a crop's code, yielding natural enhancements with minimal environmental impact.

Fulfilled and Productive Workforces	Learning Labs	With over 100 million forcibly displaced people worldwide and 1.6 million English language learners in UK schools, educators face a unique challenge. Learning Labs addresses this by providing FlashAcademy®, an AI-powered platform assessing and teaching English from forty-eight languages, helping students excel academically.
	Learnerbly	Learnerbly revolutionizes employee development through its learning marketplace, sourcing content from over 250 trusted providers, including books, podcasts, e-learning and coaching. They offer personalized learning paths, empowering individuals to drive their skill development in a changing world, fostering a culture of continuous learning.
	Reelyze	In response to the global productivity crisis, Reelyze offers a UK-based SaaS platform, providing on-the-go access to vital knowledge and training for the distributed workforce. Only 10 per cent of the global workforce has regular access to a desk and computer, meaning 90 per cent of workers are excluded from learning, development and instant access to critical information.
	Guideline	Guideline simplifies retirement planning with affordable, automated 401(k) plans, eradicating hidden fees and paperwork. Their online platform democratizes secure retirement access, especially for those previously hindered by high fees or complex options.

Healthy ageing	Mito Therapeutics	MitoRx Therapeutics leads in developing mitochondrial-modulating medicines for degenerative diseases, notably severe muscular dystrophy. It's breakthroughs target mitochondria directly, offering a transformative approach to halt muscle damage.
	Stroll	Strolll's Reality DTx software for augmented reality glasses transforms Parkinson's Disease rehabilitation, offering personalized sessions at home, easing strain on healthcare systems, and showing tangible improvements within weeks.
	Barinthus Biotherapeutics	Barinthus Biotherapeutics, formerly Vaccitech, made waves with its COVID-19 vaccine, saving 6.3 million lives in the first year of AstraZeneca's roll out during the pandemic. Now, its focus extends to combating chronic viral infections like MERS with innovative T-cell immunotherapies.
	Laverock Therapeutics	Laverock Therapeutics pioneered a gene silencing platform, GEiGS®, for advanced human therapeutics. Uniquely, it can partially up or down regulate RNA signalling and allows the fine control of engineered cells for cancer and inflammatory disease applications.

Impact Is an Important Pillar for Returns for Future Planet Capital

Addressing these global challenges was important for driving returns. Apart from his own personal inclination towards creating something meaningful, Hansen-Luke wanted to ensure that HLD Partners were creating real value. He likes to cite the example of Pokemon Go to emphasize how value can dissipate quickly if the product or service is not critical to the end consumer. Pokémon Go is a 2016 augmented reality (AR) mobile game, part of the Pokémon franchise, developed and published by Niantic, in collaboration with Nintendo and The Pokémon Company for iOS and Android devices. The game is free-to-play, using a freemium model with local advertising and in-app purchases for additional in-game items. Pokémon Go was released to mixed reviews; critics praised the concept but criticized technical problems. It was one of the most used and profitable mobile apps in 2016, having been downloaded more than 500 million times worldwide by the end of the year. It is credited with popularizing location-based and AR technology, promoting physical activity, and helping local businesses grow due to escalated foot traffic.[8] However, it drew controversy for causing accidents and public nuisances. Several governments raised security concerns, leading some countries to regulate its use. Yet, only a few months later, its grandeur faded. Seemingly forever. Its active player base evaporated. Globally, only 5 million people now play the game on a daily basis. And, despite an uptick during the pandemic, the numbers seem to be falling continuously.[9]

Hansen-Luke firmly believes that tackling the five global challenges keeps them sharp and focused on creating real value. Around the same time that Future Planet Capital identified these five focus areas (climate change, education, health, security, and sustainable growth), the United Nations had come up with Sustainable Development Goals (SDGs). The SDGs include similar areas identified by Future Capital. As a result, the company chose to communicate its focus areas by identifying its causes with the relevant SDGs listed by the United Nations. The table below represents various UN SDGs, addressed by each of the funds managed by Future Planet Capital.

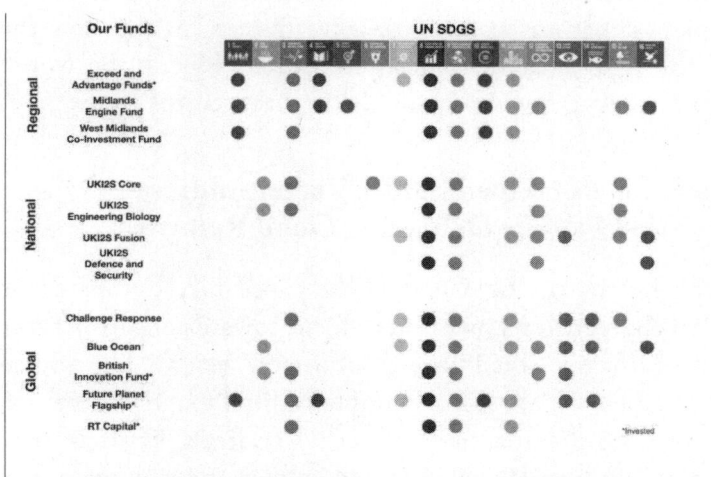

Figure 14: UN SDGs addressed by different funds managed by future planet

To summarize, health accounts for the largest share of Future Planet Capital's investments, with 34.2 per cent of their portfolio, working towards improving health and well-being (SDG 3). Meanwhile, 16.4 per cent of their investments address a climate-related goal (SDGs 7,11,12,13,14 and 15) while 20.5 per cent of their portfolio are trying to improve socio-economic well-being and economic growth (SDG 8). A focus on deep tech has resulted in 16 per cent of their portfolio being aligned to industry, innovation and infrastructure (SDG 9).

Within the five broad areas, Future Planet Capital has identified a list of '100 Greatest Challenges' to target and source companies solving challenges in these areas. According to Future Planet Capital, over thirty-five of the challenges, from decarbonizing road transport to chronic obstructive pulmonary disease, are problems worth over USD 100 billion. They have built these into their scoring system to link business models to these challenges. This helps them identify the next wave of companies that are working to solve these with the view that with the right business model, companies solving the world's biggest challenges will provide the highest returns.

Impact Focus Helped Future Planet Address COVID-19 While Delivering Good Returns

At the height of the COVID-19 pandemic, Future Planet Capital sharpened its investment focus towards ensuring access to safe, effective, quality and affordable essential medicines and vaccines for all. This culminated in their investment in Barinthus Biotherapeutics (formerly Vaccitech) in 2020. After investing, Future Planet Capital helped the company raise USD 43m in convertible notes and then a further USD 168m in the Series B and IPO. The impact was profound: Barinthus's technology delivered over three billion vaccines across more than 180 countries, saving 6.3 million lives in the first year of roll out, during the pandemic.

Future Planet Has Developed a Quantitative Framework to Assess Impact

Future Planet Capital believes that with the right business model, positive impacts on people and planet drive outsized returns. If innovative companies can solve pressing issues, they will be rewarded, as will their investors. They invest where shareholders, people and planetary interests align. Their framework for assessing impact involves calculating the Impact Value Gap (IVG). This helps frame how large a solution's potential added benefit, or reduction of cost, could be in dollar terms. It is built following industry best practice, academic research and internal expertise.

The Impact framework operates on the same premise as Fermi Estimates—logical deductive scaling. It starts with a global challenge, estimates the value in solving for it and then deduces the scale of impact a company could have. The Impact Framework is based on estimates and grounded in assumptions. As such, the final dollar value is less important, but rather it is the scale and the narrative of how a company can have an impact which takes precedence. Whilst negative externalities are important considerations and are recognized elsewhere in their investment decisions, this framework identifies and sizes positive impact potential.

The exhibit below shows how the Impact Value Gap tool works in practice.

Impact Value Gap (IVG) tool helps them gauge the size of the potential impact as they aim to invest in solutions that have the broadest or deepest impact. It gives them a rough idea of how big an impact a solution could have in dollar terms, making it easier to understand how scalable and globally applicable it is. Additionally, it shows them the value of addressing key challenges and lets them compare it with financial valuations to see if societal value is integrated into business models. FPC believes that it's important to keep them accountable for investing in the most impactful companies while helping them focus their investment team's efforts. The IVG allows comparison across different investment options, making decision-making clearer for their Investment Committees.

Company	Queen of Raw
Description	Queen of Raw (QoR) provides a no-code software platform to intelligently resell, recycle or reuse the USD 120 billion worth of excess fabrics and finished garments that are typically disposed of each year.
Step 1 Identify Impact Pathways. Finding a figure for the benefit or cost of the problem a company is trying to solve. This is linked to anchor studies, pilot reports, primary research, independent and accredited third-party bodies or peer reviewed journals. The IVG is per annum—a one-time figure for a one-time stage investment.	**Pathway 1:** The global textiles industry is responsible for 3.3gT of Carbon Emissions p.a.[10] 15 per cent of textiles end up on the cutting room floor as waste.[11] 3.3gT x 0.15 = 495mT CO2e apportioned to waste in the textile industry. IMF price of CO2 per tonne required by 2030 = USD 75.[12] USD 75 x 495mT = USD 37.125bn **Pathway 2:** Global textiles industry = 20 per cent of clean water pollution. Clean water pollution[13] reduces GDP of developing countries by 0.82 per cent.[14] GDP of all developing countries = USD 42tn.[15] 15 per cent of textiles end up on the cutting room floor as waste. [16] USD 42000bn x 0.0082 x 0.2 x 0.15 = USD 10.33bn

Step 2	When investing they were operating
Determine the increase or reduction in the benefit or cost of a company's solution, given efficacy rates. This is on an assumption that the company will scale and successfully get to market.	on the assumption that Queen of Raw's MateriaMX can reduce this waste by up to 50 per cent. With the most recent pilots with Ralph Lauren showing 92 per cent landfill waste reduction, their assumption was conservative.
Step 3	
In this step they determine the IVG figure. They can then take this figure and apply three variables to get a more tailored figure given the stage or maturity of a company—the time to impact, an internal discount and the likelihood of success. These are all based on industry analysis and corroborated by their own pipeline.	Emissions Pathway 1: USD 37.16bn x 0.5 = USD 18.58bn Water Pollution Pathway 2: USD 10.33bn x 0.5 = USD 5.17bn Total IVG—Pathway 1 + Pathway 2: USD 23.75 billion

Figure 15: Assessing the impact value gap for Queen of Raw

Data at the Core of Investment Process

Future Planet's investment process is unique. They have access to many innovative companies and ideas emerging from top universities. So, they have created a data-driven algorithm to evaluate the companies. Their platform tracks over 1900 companies, using more than 5,00,000 data points, to evaluate emerging investment opportunities from leading research and innovation ecosystems. This enables their investment teams to prioritize promising companies in breakthrough sectors, from RNA vaccines to nuclear fusion reactors, irrespective of originating university.

Each pipeline company is assigned a score based on the over thirty features they evaluate. These consider the track record of a company, scale of the commercial opportunity, strength of their links to their university ecosystems and the scale of positive impact they aim to create. These four components are combined to create an overarching Future Planet Investment Score, from 0–100 to reflect their percentile within their pipeline. Underpinning this approach is an extensive review of academic literature to identify characteristics that have had a strong empirical link to success in the past. This enables Future Planet Capital to differentiate between signals that have consistently indicated success across investment cycles and industry features that lack an empirical basis.

Addressing Climate Change

This approach of identifying and investing in solutions addressing the biggest problems has led Future Planet Capital to invest in Tokamak Energy, which aims to develop commercial fusion energy for global deployment in the 2030s. In his book, *How to Avoid a Climate Disaster*, Bill Gates states that the key solution to avoid a climate disaster is to convert everything to electric power (e.g. automobiles) and make electricity from renewable sources. However, he mentions that solar and wind energy are not efficient renewable sources because of their high land use. Hence, according to Gates, we do not have enough land to get all our electricity from these sources. The solution that could make a difference is nuclear energy—especially energy generated by nuclear fusion. This might require some explanation.

Nuclear fission is the process that regular nuclear reactors work on which involves taking very heavy atoms such as uranium and splitting those into smaller atoms to release their energy. Fusion, on the other hand, takes very light atoms, for example, hydrogen, and fuses those together to form slightly heavier elements, such as helium. Fusion is the process that powers the sun and the stars in the universe. In the very hot and dense conditions in the center of the sun, the ions are being forced together with tremendous force such that they bond together and form these helium nuclei and release energy. This is facilitated by the incredible gravitational force that sun has to create dense conditions that make this reaction occur readily.

On Earth, we don't have powerful gravity. That's why exceptionally powerful electromagnets are needed to generate the forces required. In addition, temperatures around ten times hotter than the center of the sun are required to achieve fusion on Earth. To achieve such high temperatures, a vacuum chamber surrounded by powerful magnets which are designed to confine superheated plasma without touching the chamber's walls (otherwise it would melt) is needed. The chamber is called *Tokamak*.

Fusion represents the holy grail for energy production. It offers us the potential of abundant energy produced in a safe manner without radioactive waste or carbon emissions. Hence, the solutions developed by Tokamak Energy could be the key contributor to achieving net zero targets and limiting climate change. Tokamak Energy's ability to achieve a landmark plasma ion temperature in excess of 100 million degrees Celsius, considered the threshold for commercial fusion, has significantly improved the probability of success.

Fusion research in the United Kingdom continued after the Second World War ended. Several universities, including Oxford and Imperial College, contributed to the research. In 1965, the United Kingdom Atomic Energy Authority created a laboratory in Culham, just south of Oxford, as a purpose-built home for Britain's fusion research program. Tokamak Energy was spun out of the UK Atomic Energy Authority in 2009 by three cofounders—Alan Sykes, Mikhail Gryaznevich and David Kingham. Future Planet Capital invested half a million in the Company by 2015. Since then, the Company has raised USD 250 million. While Future Planet Capital is well positioned at an attractive IRR based on the most recent valuation round, this company still has a long way to go in terms of building a commercial solution. However, when Tokamak solves the nuclear fusion puzzle, it will unlock abundant clean energy and help us move away from fossil fuels and greenhouse gas emissions and, in turn, address the biggest challenge in climate change problem. It will also likely lead to significant returns for Future Planet Capital.

Building Retirement Solutions for Excluded Population

Complex research from universities are not the only ideas that Future Planet funds. They also invest in addressing the large socio-economic challenges of our time. A great example of solving a socio-economic problem at scale is Guideline, which simplifies retirement planning with affordable, automated plans, eliminating hidden fees and paperwork. Their online platform democratizes secure retirement access, especially for those previously hindered by high fees or complex options.

Guideline was founded by Kevin Busque in 2017 after he sold TaskRabbit, a business he cofounded with his wife Leah, to Ikea. TaskRabbit operates an online marketplace that allows people to find freelance labour offering furniture assembly, delivery and handyman work. Guideline's idea was borne out of the pain faced by Kevin while handling the human resource function at TaskRabbit. While the large organizations were chased by fund managers, there were hardly any firms advising small businesses on how to handle the retirement plans for their employees. Kevin started work on offering the 401(k)[17] plan, which is an employer sponsored, defined contribution personal pension account in the United States.

By enabling consistent saving and financial stability, the company empowers individuals and communities, facilitating sustainable long-term savings. By the end of 2023, Guideline's streamlined approach attracted over 47,000 businesses, solidifying their leadership in the affordable pension plan market, with over USD 12 billion saved for retirement and significantly reduced fee costs. Future Planet invested USD 1.4 million in Guideline in Series B. Since their investment, the company has attracted leading investors such as General Atlantic, Tiger Global and NEA, raising more than USD 300 million. At the last round valuation, Future Planet's stake is valued at 5.8x of its investment.

Exits and Unicorns

Investing in these innovative companies has led to a strong return profile for the Fund. Future Planet has already witnessed eight portfolio companies, including those invested in by its founders, become unicorns, a term used to signify companies valued at more than USD 1 billion.

Hansen-Luke believes that the real returns are yet to reflect. Events like the success of Tokamak Energy and IPO of Guideline will massively change the returns. They will make a huge difference to society as well. In his journey to help high-quality innovations secure the capital and support needed to tackle the world's biggest challenges, Hansen-Luke knows this is just the beginning.

10

Lok Capital: Driving Financial Inclusion in India

Serendipity played a major role in Vishal Mehta's life. In 1999, after having worked for four years in the telecom sector in India, he decided to do an MBA from Stephen M. Ross School of Business at the University of Michigan in the United States. When he began studying for his degree, he had a clear vision: to either make a professional shift into the consultancy space or continue in the telecom sector. This was the time that India's privatization story had just about started, and many new private ventures were being set-up across sectors including financial services, telecom, education and healthcare. Up until that time, most of these services and their delivery was dominated by government run and controlled institutions. Vishal's job in the telecom space in India was a direct result of this privatization story where he also very quickly realized that most of these new ventures were being set up for the higher income segment in India and for the masses the life wasn't really changing much. This realization of non-inclusive growth that he was witnessing was buried somewhere down in his priorities and did not get exposed until he got to University of Michigan.

But when he began his studies at the University of Michigan, he took a course that would, quite literally, change his life. The course was taught by C.K. Prahalad, then one of the world's most visionary management thinkers. Prahalad had been teaching at Michigan Ross since 1981, but his influence grew in 2004 when he co-authored a book titled *The Fortune at the Bottom of the Pyramid*. The book galvanized how multi-national corporations (MNCs) across the world looked at dealing with the poorest consumers. In itself, 'bottom of the pyramid' was not a new concept. It had first been used by the US President, Frankin D. Roosevelt, in 1932, when he talked about poor people who were often forgotten, because they lived at the bottom of the economic pyramid.[1] This demographic segment, argued Prahalad, was actually a profitable consumer base. As he explained, ' . . . typical pictures of poverty mask the fact that the very poor represent resilient entrepreneurs and value-conscious consumers.'[2] In his opinion, what was needed was a better, more empathetic approach to help the very poor— one that involved partnering with them to drive innovation and to create sustainable scenarios where they remained actively engaged while companies profitably provided products and services. 'Large-scale and wide-spread entrepreneurship is at the heart of the solution to poverty.' Prahalad wrote: 'Such an approach exists and has, in several instances, gone well past the idea stage as private enterprises, both large and small, have begun to successfully build markets at the bottom of the pyramid (BOP) as a way of eradicating poverty.'[3]

This would mean that a formula would have to be created to achieve optimum results. Prahalad devised a 'low price, low margin, high volume' model; products could be offered at very low prices and margins, to generate profits simply by selling in enormous quantities. This model changed management strategies almost permanently. In India, the greatest example was Hindustan Unilever's success in selling the Wheel brand of detergent to low-income consumers in India.

Prahalad wasn't a very flamboyant speaker. There were no antics on stage, and he spoke with almost no expressiveness or voice modulation. But when he did speak, it always left a profound impact on those who were listening to him.[4] This was exactly the effect on Vishal. This totally resonated with the lack of inclusive growth he had witnessed in his stint at private sector in India. It was perhaps serendipitous that at this same moment, he met Dr Aravind, then his senior at Michigan Ross. Aravind is the grandson of Dr Govindappa Venkataswamy, Founder and former chairman of Aravind Eye Care chain of hospitals,[5] and was involved with the hospital chain, focused on addressing the needs of low and middle-income people in India. As Vishal spent time with Aravind, he began to think along the lines of what he had heard Prahalad discuss in class. One of the first opportunities to test these ideas was the possibility of replicating Aravind Eye Care's model in Africa (the model was already functioning well in India) as part of one of his elective courses during his MBA. It was the first time that Vishal was thinking actively of a business model where profit maximization was not the objective, and where shareholder value was seen in a very different way.

His experiences convinced Vishal that his interests lay not in the telecom sector as he had once thought, but in the social sector. But practicality intervened. He had to still pay off his student loans, so for the next couple of years, Vishal worked at Capital One, a consulting firm in Washington DC. Then, he began to actively scout for new opportunities in the social space. Almost a year passed. Unfortunately, the traditional non-profit sector was looking for vintage and sector expertise—the one thing that Vishal lacked, since he was from a fairly commercial mainstream business background. As nearly every opportunity hit a dead end, once again, serendipity took the wheel.

It was around this time that Rajiv Lall moved to New York. Lall was then a managing partner at Warburg Pincus, one of the world's largest private equity firms. Lall wanted to use the same principle of venture capital for socially relevant businesses. He wanted to put his significant experience in investment to use in India, the one country where he felt this model would be not only viable but successful. Naturally, then, he was looking for someone who would be able to drive this cause forward and be based out of India.

Rajiv heard about Vishal from a common acquaintance. He liked what he heard and gave Vishal a cold call, which reached his voice mail. As he listened to Lall's voice message, Vishal quickly did some preliminary research on Warburg Pincus,[6] as he was totally unaware of the private equity industry. Soon, the two set up a meeting over coffee.

It was serendipity once more. After a three-hour long meeting, Vishal was ready to move back to India and get to work (on almost a quarter of the salary he was earning) to build Lall's vision. The two men had even come up with a name: Lok Capital. Delighted, Lall asked him to discuss matters with his wife before making any kind of firm commitment. Vishal laughed and said, 'I will discuss it with her, but I'm making this commitment to you: I will move to India!'

From that day onwards, Lok Capital became Vishal's baby.

The idea behind Lok Capital was to work with social businesses and help them grow. Vishal was excited by the principles that lay behind this vision. For him, geography didn't matter. Working in the social space (the phrase 'impact investment' had not been coined back then) and making a positive change was his biggest motivation. But in hindsight, the roadmap for this wasn't too clear. In addition, he was of the view that he had underestimated his lack of experience in the investment space. And that is where Lok Capital's another key supporter, Donald Peck, stepped in.

Rajiv introduced Vishal to Donald Peck, who had spent seven to eight years in India, making private equity investments for the Commonwealth Development Corporation (CDC), which is now called the British International Investment (BII). Lall and Peck clearly had nothing to lose by sending Vishal out to India to build Lok Capital. The Lok Capital experiment had gained the support of prominent asset management professionals like Vijay Advani,[7] who retired recently as the executive chairman of Nuveen, a leading global asset management firm and prior to that was the chairman of Franklin Templeton, another large asset management firm. Advani agreed to fund some early expenses alongside Lall and Peck. This was in addition to the funds already raised by Lall, from the Rockefeller Foundation, which would be used to conduct basic groundwork and research on the kind of social enterprises that needed to be targeted and how Lok Capital could narrow the list down.

The Quest for Investors Leads to Development Finance Institutions (DFIs)

The key question for all three men remained: Who would be likely to give them the required capital? After all, these were early days. Nobody really knew what Lok Capital would be or what its model was going to look like. Lall, Peck and Vishal tried to raise a very small fund in order to make investments that could act as a proof of concept. Their first target were India's ultra-high-net individuals (HNIs). The ultra HNIs liked the concept of investing to benefit the poor and encouraged Vishal's ideas. But to his frustration, nobody was willing to commit their own capital. As a result, his efforts were unsuccessful. Nearly nine months passed slowly by, adding to his anxieties. But impact investing was too radical a concept, even for ultra HNIs. Looking back, Vishal and his team didn't make it easy on themselves. For one, they structured the fund manager (known

also as a general partner entity, or, more simply, a GP) as a
non-profit. In addition, the founders also decided to set aside
50 per cent of the carried interest[8] for the Lok Foundation.
Unsurprisingly, some investors balked at investing simply
due to the structure. But for the founders of Lok Capital, its
structure reflected their own personal principles. They wanted
to walk the same path that they requested their investors to
follow. After spending some time unsuccessfully trying to raise
money in India, they found their sweet spot with Development
Finance Institutions (DFIs) from US and Europe. And exactly
during these uncertain times, Vishal met his co-founder Venky
Natarajan and this proved to be another turning point in Lok
Capital's journey. Vishal and Venky have now worked together
for around twenty years probably the only GP in India where
co-founders have stuck along over four funds.

Soon, Vishal was joined by other like-minded individuals.
The most important was his co-founder, Venky Natarajan, who
had been working in California with Intel Capital for almost
a decade. With very similar motivations to Vishal, he was also
exploring the idea of a more meaningful professional career.
Venky had been working with an NGO called Freedom from
Hunger as an adviser. At Freedom from Hunger, microfinance
experiments had been conducted in India. This had brought
Venky to India, and on one of his trips, he met Vishal who
did not have to do much to get Venky to give up his life in the
United States and move to India to join Lok Capital.

In 2006, Vishal and his team closed the first fund at USD 22
million, with leading names such as the International Finance
Corporation (IFC), the BII (British International Investment,
then known as CDC), the FMO (Dutch Entrepreneurial
Development Bank), the KfW (German Development Bank)
and Accion (an international non-profit with a focus on
financial inclusion) as investors. Significantly, this would be the
first fund that Accion International ever committed itself to.

Microfinance Becomes the Area of Focus for the First Fund

The next step was to identify investments in line with Lok Capital's philosophy of improving the lives of people at the bottom of the income pyramid. Vishal knew that if he had to attract more capital in future, he would have to demonstrate investment returns in line with market rate returns to his investors. By now, and after in-depth research, he had also realized that to generate those market-rate returns, Lok Capital would have to use India's only sizable and consistent pipeline: the microfinance space. While a handful of exciting opportunities in the fields of healthcare and education existed, a pipeline of companies with similar social intent in these spaces was difficult to find or build. Investors also suggested that they should try to solve one problem at a time and focus only on microfinance. So, Vishal and his team decided to stick to microfinance with the intent of moving on to other areas in future.

Fund I Generates Top-Quartile Performance

The years 2006 and 2007 were ones of frenzy. The stock markets were rising almost every other day. In hindsight, those were amongst the worst vintages for private equity. In 2009, when Vishal met the CEO of BII (then known as CDC), an investor in his fund and a very prominent investor in emerging markets, he felt slightly embarrassed. After all, he would be delivering a USD IRR[9] of only USD 9-10 per cent. To Vishal's surprise, however, BII's CEO called him a hero—Lok Capital, he said, was among the best performing funds in their thirty Indian investments. Fund I had several success stories, with several investments becoming leading names in microfinance in India. Ujjivan, founded by Samit Ghosh, is one such microfinance company which later became a bank.

Ujjivan: An Accomplished Banker's Vision to Do Something Meaningful

Ghosh worked as a banker for thirty years with top banks, including HDFC Bank, Standard Chartered Bank in Dubai and Citibank in India, Dubai and Bahrain. However, he felt that his father, Dr Sailendra Kumar Ghosh, would not be too satisfied with his son's achievements. After all, Dr Ghosh had helped establish several government hospitals, rather than chasing the lure of a wealthy private practice, preferring to using his knowledge to serve those in need. Driven by this thought, the younger Ghosh set up Ujjivan, a microfinance company, in November 2005. His objective was to improve financial access for nearly 600 million working poor. He started with Rs 27 million (USD 0.6 million at that time), and out of this Rs 6 million (USD 1,30,000 at that time) had come from Ghosh's own pocket and the balance from friends and family. In line with the standard microfinance model created by Grameen Bank, Ujjivan lent money to working women who wanted to set up a small-scale business.

Samit Ghosh's vision aligned well with Vishal and Venky's own philosophies and the mandate of the fund. Lok Capital was one of the early investors in Ujjivan, investing in December 2008 from Fund I, and again from Fund II in January 2012. Post their investment, Lok Capital also helped Ujjivan raise capital from prominent investors such as the International Finance Corporation (IFC) and the British International Investment (BII). The business scaled significantly with Ujjivan increasing its customer base nearly threefold from 6,50,000 in FY2010 (i.e., the year ending March 2010) to 1.8 million in FY2015 (i.e., the year ending March 2015) while growing its Assets Under Management (AUM), more than eight times. This also translated to more than 7.5 times the growth in revenue more than nine times growth in net profit by FY2015.

The strong growth created excellent exit opportunities and healthy financial returns for Lok Capital, which sold its Fund I investment in April 2015 and its Fund II investment in June 2017, a short while after Ujjivan got its small finance bank license in November 2016. Since then, the business has only continued to grow, achieving a loan book of more than Rs 2,70,000 million (USD 3.2 billion) as of December 2023.

Fund II Delivers Top-Decile Returns

The strong performance in Fund I helped Lok Capital attract more impact investors such as TIAA, responsibility and Triple Jump. Lok Capital raised USD 64 million for Fund II in 2010. Fund II did even better and delivered USD 22 percent IRR and was in the top decile for funds of a similar vintage.

Fund II has also had several success stories, driven by the IPOs of portfolio companies, such as MAS, Equitas, Suryoday and Utkarsh, in addition to Ujjivan, in which Fund II was also an investor. In Fund II, Lok Capital diversified beyond microfinance into wider financial services and experimented with other sectors such as healthcare, education and agriculture. Veritas, a lender focused on Micro, small and medium enterprises (MSME) founded by Dr Arulmany, is a good example of their diversification within financial services.

Veritas: Supporting the Growth of MSMEs

Dr Arulmany graduated from the Institute of Rural Management (IRMA) and worked in sectors related to rural enterprises such as dairy. In 1995, he joined a reputed Non-Banking Financial Services company (NBFC) called Cholamandalam Investment and Finance Company. Here, he learned the nuances of lending, but more importantly, he gained firsthand experience of the opportunities and challenges of working in rural India. Soon, Dr Arulmany began working with stalwarts of the lending industry, such as P.N. Vasudevan and M Anandan, who later went on to establish Equitas Small Finance Bank and Aptus Value Housing, respectively. Dr Arulmany briefly joined Aptus Value Housing as president and CEO. But in 2015, he decided to launch Veritas Finance with the objective of meeting the short, medium and long-term financial requirements of the financially excluded micro and small enterprises.

During the initial days of Veritas, Dr Arulmany personally evaluated 500 borrowers and passed on his methods to his team. Over time, his insights translated into a model to evaluate customers who did not have credit ratings. Veritas' focus on addressing the needs of the MSME sector was a natural fit with Lok Capital's mandate. Lok Capital had decided to fund Veritas very early in its journey, when the business had a loan book of less than a million dollars. Lok Capital helped Dr Arulmany build a governance framework from their experience of working with leading lending institutions. They also helped the company attract new investors such as the British International Investment (BII).

Armed with the right support and capital, Veritas has evolved into one of the leaders in MSME financing in India, with nearly 400 branches, serving more than 1,70,000 MSMEs across eight states in southern and eastern India. As of March 2024, it had a loan book of more than USD 650 million and reported annual net profit of more than USD 25 million. Lok Capital sold 20 per cent of its stake, as part of one of the follow-on rounds and has already recovered more than the capital invested.

Investors such as Lok Capital were one of the key drivers, then, in facilitating the growth of microfinance in India. Their performance attracted large chunks of commercial capital to space in turn driving the long-term growth of the industry.

In 2015, when the Reserve Bank of India granted ten small finance bank licenses, eight were microfinance institutions and five out of those eight were Lok Capital investee companies, which had been backed by Lok Capital early in their individual journeys. This speaks volumes about Lok Capital's ability to identify the right people and help them build quality institutions.

While it may seem like Lok Capital got lucky, Vishal and his team spent a lot of time figuring out the right partner. They believe that this is one of the main reasons behind their success. According to Vishal, Lok partners only with people they can relate to. Specifically, they are looking for similarities between why Vishal and Venky started Lok Capital and why their partners started their own companies. Vishal believes that if they get that right, then the entrepreneurs will not do something that goes against the principles of their business and of impact investment. Operational execution and integrity have been key pillars of their investment thesis, according to Vishal. He gives 70 per cent of the weight during the deal evaluation to promoter referencing and understanding founder's motivations.

Lok Capital does not take credit for the operational excellence of their portfolio companies. According to Vishal, they help their portfolio companies, primarily in three areas: a) Helping promoters find the right team as they grow. That's where their network plays a very important role. b) Helping their partners raise money because that's what they haven't done before. For every dollar invested by Lok Capital, they have been able to attract 2.5 dollars from their investors in the same rounds in the same companies. c) Helping them with technology. They focus a lot on ensuring a strong relationship with the founder and the management team. Several of Lok Capital's portfolio companies turn to them for advice, even after they have completely exited and are no longer an investor.

Lok Capital's success over the years has been driven by three important factors:

a) Partnering with the right entrepreneurs
b) Adding value to their portfolio and
c) Relentless focus on exits.

Experiments in Education and Healthcare

After its success with financial inclusion, Lok Capital experimented with education and healthcare in Fund II. In 2012, they invested in the Karnataka-based rural education provider, Hippocampus Learning Centres (HLC). It was their first investment in the education sector, but even though the founders were rated highly by Vishal, Lok Capital soon realized that HLC was not going to generate commercial returns. In Vishal's words: 'We realized that it's very hard to create commercials returns in education with a focus on bottom of the pyramid, especially in a venture timeframe, i.e., over five years. If you have a very liberal definition of impact on education, you can still make it work. But if you want to be focused on bottom of the pyramid, then within five years with that price point, you just can't commercialize.'

Their healthcare experience, on the other hand, was encouraging. However, Vishal felt that even if he did have large sums to deploy in healthcare, it would be hard for Lok to consistently find good opportunities. The scale of the impact was impressive with Fund II portfolio companies reaching out to serving 11.5 million low and middle-income borrowers, 85 per cent of them being women, 5,00,000 patients and 3500 farmers.

Lok Capital Experiments with More Sectors in Fund III

Driven by its strong performances in Fund II, Lok Capital raised USD 90 million for Fund III, which was topped up to USD 105 million in the wake of the COVID-19 pandemic, as Lok Capital sought additional capital from their investors to support their portfolio companies. Financial services and especially unsecured lending—dependent on micro enterprises—were significantly impacted due to the lockdown in India.

In Fund III, while Lok Capital continued to focus on financial inclusion, it also invested in companies such as the supply chain financing platform, Mintifi, which leveraged technology to further drive inclusion.

Mintifi: Leveraging Technology for Driving Inclusion

Anup Agarwal, the founder of Mintifi, was a managing director at Jeffries, where he covered the evolving telecom, media and technology sectors. In 2017, he decided to take a plunge into entrepreneurship and set up Mintifi, along with his friend Ankit Mehta. Their vision was to address the cash-flow challenges of small and medium enterprises (SMEs).

Agarwal invested half a million dollars of his own capital to fund the initial tech. In time, Mintifi developed an innovative model, by creating a win-win model in partnership with large corporates. It leveraged the supply chain relationships and transaction data of these corporates to offer loans to their distributors and retailers, which, in turn, helped their businesses grow. In the process, worthy small and medium enterprises were able to raise funds at a much lower rate compared to market rates. Meanwhile, Mintifi not only improved its ability to underwrite these SMEs but also significantly reduced origination and collection costs by leveraging corporate partnerships.

In September 2017, Lok Capital infused a seed round of USD 2 million into Mintifi. Lok Capital had been looking to invest in FinTech models and was excited by the potential of a fundamentals-focused, differentiated lending business, led by capable and aligned founders. The supply chain financing product improved access to credit for small and medium businesses, which were (and are) starved for credit, and were not served by formal banks.

Post Lok's funding, the team brought on board Sanjoy, who had significant experience in risk, to join as a co-founder. From then onwards, Anup and his team have not looked back. Through its digital platform, Mintifi has been able to swiftly access MSME entrepreneurs across India. Today, the platform serves customers in every state of India and has provided working capital financing to over 20,800 borrowers across industries. Lok Capital played a key role in advising the company on its portfolio diversification strategy, helping set up governance and reporting systems, making key hires, raising capital and introducing Mintifi to new channel partners.

In May 2018, Mintifi raised USD 16 million—a figure which increased to USD 40 million in February 2022 and to USD 110 million in March 2023. These increases were driven by significant business growth, with disbursements of USD 1.7 billion in FY23 (year ending March 2023), generating revenues of over USD 150 million and profits of USD 10 million. This is extremely rare in the tech world, where most companies do not reach profitability until many years after achieving the unicorn status.

Lok Capital invested a total of USD 10 million, including a seed in 2017, a follow on in 2019 and then a bridge round in 2021, to help buffer the uncertainty of the pandemic. Since then, Lok Capital has achieved attractive returns by selling down some of its stakes, during the follow-on fundraises.

The company is continuously improving its products, offering to support many more MSMEs in their growth journey, as it scales further and plans eventually to list an IPO.

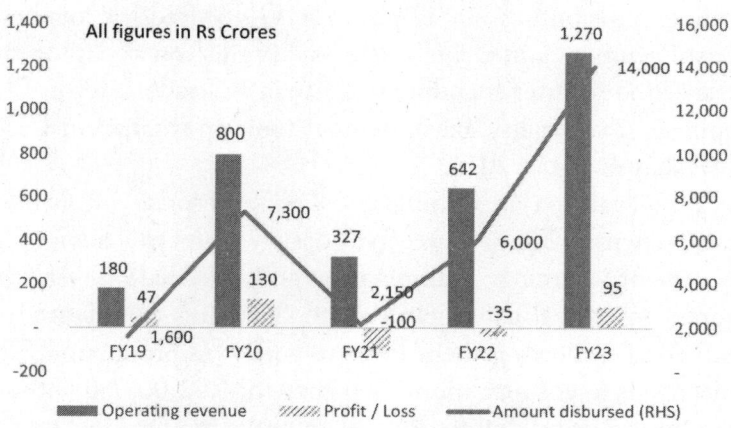

Figure 16: Mintifi financial performance

Source: 'Title of the Article', Forbes India,
https://www.forbesindia.com/printcontent/90757

Lok Capital has continued to experiment with other sectors, which has resulted in successes, such as Renewbuy in insurance and Akshayakalpa in dairy.

Akshayakalpa: Increasing Dairy Farmers Incomes by 5x

Dr Guddahatti Nanjunda Srinivas (GNS) Reddy, a veterinarian, was deeply inspired after a lecture by Dr Manibhai Desai, the founder of Bharatiya Agro-Industries Foundation (BAIF), which pioneered rural development in India. Dr Reddy worked with BAIF for nearly two decades, focusing on innovations in forestry, irrigation and watershed management. However, due to certain constraints, he was not able to incubate an organic dairy and farming model within BAIF. In 2010, he moved out of BAIF to establish Akshayakalpa, which means 'endless possibilities' in Hindi. Dr GNS Reddy's nephew, Shashi Kumar, joined his uncle in his mission to uplift the rural economy after spending more than a decade as a software engineer. Eventually, Shashi Kumar took up the role of CEO at Akshayakalpa in 2016.

Akshayakalpa is envisaged as an enterprise of farmer-entrepreneurs. Farmers receive design support, advice on equipment sourcing, maintenance and vaccination services, trained in animal care, helped with financing and assured of marketing—allowing them to focus solely on production. The objective is to ensure a monthly income of Rs 1,00,000 without the physical grind that traditional dairying and farming entails, so that youth are incentivized to remain in villages, rather than being forced to migrate to cities.

According to the National Survey of Milk Adulteration in 2011, as much as 70 per cent of the milk sold in the market is adulterated. As the dairy system focuses on quantity versus quality, it often overlooks the health of the cows, a prime factor in producing good quality milk. Cows are tied up in congested areas, limiting their freedom to graze in the fields. Instead, they are fed with factory-made fodder, such as groundnut cakes, and are also injected with steroids and artificial hormones, which increase productivity, but the harmful chemicals surface in the milk that is produced. Dr Reddy believed that the pasteurization process destroy many vital elements such as Vitamin A, B6, B12, calcium and iodine.

Akshayakalpa uses technology to automate the entire dairy farm, eliminating human touch and minimizing the risk of diseases. Its model requires an investment of Rs 2–2.5 million per shed, which is enough to purchase 20–25 cows, an advanced cowshed, an automated milking system, a fodder chopper and chilling unit and a bio-gas plant and a generator. It places great emphasis on the cows' health. Cows are free to gaze at their own will. Their sheds are cleaned regularly, limiting the risk of diseases. Every single cow is monitored electronically and regularly for its health and overall milk production. In addition, cows are given a mix of organic fodder; monocots (maize, ragi and local jowar) and dicots (cow pea and velvet beans) along with tree fodder (moringa), all of which are grown organically by the farmers themselves. Everything from milking the cow to chilling the milk produced is handled by machines without human contact, eliminating the need for pasteurization completely.

Lok Capital Builds In-Depth Impact Measurement Tools for Microfinance

Along with excellent financial performance, Lok Capital's portfolio companies have reached more than ten million beneficiaries, helping them access quality yet affordable products and services. Lok Capital measures impact through its own framework called Social Action Plan since using a framework like IRIS[10] would give a good score to all their portfolio companies, which are largely focused on microfinance. Lok Capital doesn't look at simplified frameworks or metrics like the percentage of women. Because in microfinance, nearly 99 per cent of the consumers are women. Instead, their framework Social Action Plan goes to the next level, considering factors like interaction level, training, protection and incentives offered to employees.

According to Vishal, in microfinance, once you take care of customer protection and financial literacy, the biggest stakeholders are the employees. Microfinance companies have thousands of employees who travel on motorbikes or cycles to reach customers. As a result, there are a lot of robberies, accidents and deaths on a weekly basis. So, Lok Capital's Social Action Plan also evaluates whether the company provides full health insurance and accident insurance to these employees and makes helmets compulsory for its employees.

Lok Capital also gets all its associates trained on ESG, so that they do not have to outsource ESG and impact-related work. All investment professionals are responsible for it. It also helps them evaluate ESG and impact authentically.

A Generous Pot for Foundation to Create a Bigger Impact

Today, after having delivered over thirty exits including 5 IPOs, Lok Capital is among the best performing private equity funds in India. As per data from Cambridge Associates, it is among India's top five private equity funds. Thanks to this outperformance, Lok Foundation, which receives 50 per cent of the carried interest, has now accumulated a generous pot. Vishal and Venky use this pot to support social initiatives, which they believe would not meet the return thresholds of their investors.

Fund IV and Beyond

Lok Capital has recently closed their Fund IV. It now plans to expand into new sectors with this fund. It stands as a great example of how commercial returns are possible in financial services while delivering social goods. Vishal believes that similar trends are now beginning in other sectors such as food, agriculture and climate. He hopes Lok Capital can replicate its success in these sectors.

11

Quona Capital: The Fintech Revolution

Quona Capital is a global venture firm focused on inclusive fintech. Established in 2015, Quona invests in start-ups, expanding access to financial services for consumers and businesses across India and south-east Asia, Latin America, Africa and the Middle East. It focuses on markets that are massively underserved by the legacy finance infrastructure with a large opportunity for transformation into more equitable financial systems. Beyond pure-play fintechs, Quona invests in start-ups solving broader economic and social challenges where embedded financial solutions can serve as a catalyst—from supply chain and agtech platforms to e-commerce and health. Quona has invested more than USD 600 million in more than seventy companies to date.

But it was a while before the company reached this stage.

It all began with Monica Brand Engel.

Born in Chicago, Engel spent her early years in Peru, followed by teen years in a New York suburb in Central New Jersey. Her father worked in licensing, with a focus on brands that are household names today—like *Sesame Street* and Hanna–Barbara. Her mother, a native of Peru, struggled to fit into the culture shock that was America. From each of them, Monica learned different things—her father's shrewd entrepreneurial instincts and her mother's sensitivities about her immigrant status. From a young age, Monica was aware of the importance of inclusion. When she was older, she had a chance to make the best use of that quality when it was time to apply to college. But by then, tragedy had struck.

Monica lost her mother at the age of fifteen, leaving her to look after her three younger siblings. It was a challenging time for her. She had to learn how to multitask and prioritize what was important. Her mother's illness and subsequent passing had made it clear to young Monica that what was most important was the ability to provide for oneself and one's family. At Williams College, she found inspirational professors who matched her burgeoning interests in development. She had many questions even then: why did some emerging markets do better than others? What were some of the practical challenges in making financial inclusion a reality? Her degree provided some of the answers, but not all.

After she graduated, Engel began writing case studies for Harvard Business School. She didn't particularly relish the job, but she knew that it was her first real chance to find answers to the questions she had been thinking about all through college. She knew academia wasn't the route she would take to find those answers, but the job did lead her to meet two adjunct professors at the John F. Kennedy School for Public Policy. They were studying attempts to bring microfinance—then an emerging market innovation—to underserved Latino communities in the United States. Today, we understand microfinance differently. Since the concept first came to the world's attention, it has come a long way. But in those days, when Monica began studying about it, microfinance was an idea that functioned almost entirely on trust. Still, it seemed to be an effective model for a more innovative private-sector approach to problem-solving.

Inspired by her learnings, Monica left Boston soon after and headed to Silicon Valley, where she began work in the alternative lending space with banks and community development financial institutions (CDFIs) in the Bay Area. She would spend seven years here, her first real experience, working with overlooked and underserved consumers. While she enjoyed her job, she still wanted to fulfil her desire of working internationally and that pushed her to apply to the Stanford Graduate School of Business.

From Stanford, she was recruited by McKinsey and sent to Johannesburg, and later migrated to Cape Town, where she went to work for a venture firm focused on previously disadvantaged businesses. She was happy in Cape Town, but life had other ideas for her.

One day, a friend in Washington sent her a posting that she thought would be perfect for Monica: a job with Accion, focused on bringing new product innovations to retail financial institutions in emerging markets that were serving informal microenterprises. Monica wouldn't have gone, had the then president of Accion, Michael Chu, told her something that made her sit up. Chu told her truthfully that the world—capital markets especially—could not afford to be patient with global problems like poverty. It was an excellent thing to tell Monica, for whom finding practical solutions for pressing problems like poverty was vital. In 1999, Monica Brand Engel joined Accion. It was the dawn of the new millennium, and she was responsible for product innovation. A few years in, she moved to Mexico to work directly with one of Accion's portfolio companies, Compartamos—then the largest microfinance institution in Latin America. The move was driven by her desire to work more closely with the kind of institutions and markets she was looking to help. Monica helped Compartamos develop new products in individual lending, housing finance, insurance and savings accounts.

In 2008, led by a desire to explore new technologies that were emerging in response to the financial crisis that year, Engel began to explore other options. That year, she set up Frontier Investment Group within Accion.

Monica's Vision for Quona Capital Gets Investor Interest

A few years later, Monica proposed launching a third-party fund, when there was interest from JP Morgan and Nuveen. After all, she mused, that was what had brought her to Accion originally—to mobilize the world's capital markets for the benefits of the majority. Knowing she needed partners with tech start-up experience and a solid venture track record, Engel brought on Jonathan Whittle—followed by Ganesh Rengaswamy six months later—as co-founders.

This was the beginning of Quona Capital.

Whittle was a good choice. The son of a missionary who worked across El Salvador and Costa Rica, Whittle's younger years had taught him that access to basic infrastructure was the key for aspirational classes in emerging markets. To compete globally, they needed equal access to the same tools available worldwide. As a result, the first three companies Whittle helped establish were focused on democratizing access to telecommunications services, particularly for small businesses.[1]

Yet he wasn't really exposed to financial services until he joined a private equity firm called Darby, where he managed a venture fund for Latin America. At Darby, Whittle invested in a number of different technology sectors. Two of his investments were in the financial services space, providing mobile top-up and access to prepaid products through agent networks in Mexico and Brazil. Through the network of investors, he began meeting other like-minded entrepreneurs. The more he talked to them, the more attracted he was to the idea of becoming one himself. In 2011, Whittle left Darby and—with the help of a fellow entrepreneur—he established Acesso, one of the largest prepaid telecom companies in Brazil.

After three years as CEO of Acesso, Whittle decided to return to investing, joining Accion in early 2014 to partner with Monica to raise Quona's first fund.[2]

Along with him, came Ganesh Rengaswamy. Monica had met him several times while Ganesh was working with Unitus and Lok Capital. Originally from Infosys, Ganesh had come out to the United States, driven by the desire to build something of his own. He was not in the VC space then. He knew that he needed to have the right foundation in order to be successful as a VC or founder. After working for a few years, Ganesh applied and was accepted into Harvard Business School. While he was there, he founded Travelguru. To his own shock and pleasant surprise, the company became one of the largest hotel consolidators and travel commerce companies in India and south-east Asia. Eventually, he sold it to Travelocity and Expedia, but as a learning curve, there couldn't have been a better starting point.

Over the next several years, Ganesh worked his way through venture capital. He helped lead the entry of Greylock Partners, a Silicon Valley-based venture capital fund, into the Asian/Indian market. For him, as for millions of others, the global financial crisis of 2008 was a turning point. In Ganesh's eyes, it was now or never. He began by launching an exploration into the theme of financial inclusion, initially as the Asia Director for Unitus, then as a General Partner at Lok Capital. Between these two firms, he gained experience in managing eight of the top ten microfinance institutions in India and south-east Asia. This eventually led to his joining hands with Engel and Whittle at Accion in order to incubate Quona Capital, the first emerging markets-only fintech VC.

While Monica and Jonathan were based in Washington and focused on Africa and Latin American markets, Ganesh built the office in Bengaluru to focus on the broader Asian opportunity. Initially, they got support from Accion as the company decided to spin out part of its portfolio and give it to Quona for management. Accion also committed slightly more than 15 per cent of their Fund I. Quona was the first fund to focus on digitization to drive financial inclusion and the founders felt that it was going to be a challenging exercise to raise capital. Monica and her team reached out to several DFIs and to their surprise, they found significant support for their idea to leverage technology to drive financial inclusion. In the initial days, the bigger challenge was addressing the disbelief that commercial returns can be delivered. There were also a lot of questions on what these financial inclusion business models will look like if not microfinance. Quona has seventy portfolio companies now and not a single microfinance company in line with what the founders promised their investors. But back then it was a significant effort to paint that picture and stretch the imagination of investors on what models could be possible. While it needed a lot of effort, they ended up raising USD 142 million for Fund I, which was more than the USD 100 million they set as target for themselves. It helped that all three founders had backgrounds in technology. They were able to provide a good perspective of what these financial inclusion business models would look like. A lot of effort was also needed to convince investors about the commercial feasibility of such businesses.[3]

Investment Strategy: Innovation for Inclusion

Monica, Ganesh and Jonathan always looked at financial innovation or fintech as a catalyst for broader impact. According to Ganesh, 'It was never about finance for the sake of finance, like how can you build a better trading system or core banking system or POS[4] device. It was more about how a POS solution can revolutionize retail for a small SME, which is what Yoco does in Africa. Or how can a more effective financing enable SME commerce.'[5] They picked fintech because of its ability to make an impact across multiple sectors. Today verticalized finance or embedded finance is a pretty big theme for Quona across multiple sectors, and there are likely to be a lot of crossover or hybrid solutions. Quona has portfolio companies at the cross section of mobility and fintech, agtech and fintech, food tech and fintech, healthcare and fintech and supply chain and fintech. Wherever financial innovation can be part of enabling a more comprehensive solution to catalyze a sector, and digitize the sector, it's of interest to Quona. However, the outcomes are not always very clear. As Ganesh says, 'Sometimes it's more evident when we invest, sometimes it's less evident. But if we are excited about the possibilities, we are willing to take some chances.'[6]

The Fund I made twenty investments across several fintech subsectors. In hindsight, they were investing behind the themes that would become buzzwords in five to ten years. Creditas in Brazil which went on to be funded by Softbank is a good example.

Creditas: Reducing Cost of Loans in Brazil

Sergio Furio, the founder of Creditas, joined Deutsche Bank in Spain after completing his MBA in 2000. After five years, he joined Boston Consulting Group (BCG) and focused on consulting retail banks. He moved to New York in 2008, where he worked on technology transformation projects for banks. It was an excellent decision, as Sergio recognized that technology would play a significant role in the banking sector. However, it was a conversation with his girlfriend, who is now his wife, that led to his entrepreneurial journey. He learned that Brazilians pay exorbitant interest rates, sometimes as much 200 per cent per annum, for personal loans. It sparked his curiosity, and he researched and figured that it was, in fact, true. His research revealed that high interest rates weren't driven by high funding costs for banks or expensive loans but by an extensive yet inefficient branch network, leading to higher operating costs and, in turn, steeper borrowing rates for customers.

In 2012, he moved to Brazil, with the objective of solving this problem by leveraging technology. He realized that a lot of Brazilians own assets such as car and home which do not have any loans against them but still end up taking personal loans at very high interest rates. Almost 75 per cent of Brazilians owned a home and nearly 70 per cent of those homes had no mortgage. There was a similar situation with cars. Creditas started by offering home equity loans and auto equity loans, helping customers reduce the interest burden by leveraging their assets. Over time, Creditas also started offering early salary loans and offered two salary advances free every year. These products turned out to be huge success stories with Creditas growing rapidly and reaching a loan book of more than a billion dollars by December 2023. Quona invested about USD 8 million in Creditas across several rounds. Post investment, Quona helped Creditas in several areas including strategy and fundraising which helped it evolve into one of the most successful fintech companies in Brazil and was christened a unicorn in Dec 2020 when it raised USD 255 million in a funding round led by Lightrock.[7]

Indiamart: The Lifeblood of Indian MSMEs

Quona has been willing to experiment beyond traditional financial services. This openness is reflected in their investment in Indiamart. They saw it as an opportunity for Quona to help Indiamart address the financing needs of its customers. Indiamart is one of the longest-standing B2B commerce platforms in India. The company raised two institutional funding rounds before it went public. This is unheard of amongst digital commerce companies in India, which usually take very large amounts of capital in their attempts to create value. In 2016, Ganesh led the Series B investment in Indiamart. At the time, Indiamart had been quietly building for fifteen years. In the three-plus years since Quona's initial investment, IndiaMART's user base grew to over 100 million registered businesses. In mid-2019, Indiamart went public, in a massively anticipated IPO, which was subscribed thirty-six times. In fact, it is one of the few tech stocks in India which has seen a significant increase in its share price post listing.

Success stories such as Creditas and Indiamart led to strong returns for Fund I and helped Quona raise USD 200 million for Fund II, again more than their target of USD 150 million. By Fund II, Quona started exploring the intersection of fintech with various subsectors such as healthcare, agriculture and climate. Arya, an integrated grain commerce platform that focuses on post-harvest services, is one such company that leverages fintech solutions to deliver value for farmers.

Arya: Helping Smallholder Farmers Maximize the Value of Their Produce

Arya helps smallholder farmers maximize the value of their harvest by offering warehousing and financing and helping them access the buyers without middlemen. It was founded by Prasanna Rao, Anand Chandra and Chattanathan Devarajan, each of whom has more than a decade of experience across agri-business and agri-finance.

The founders worked together at ICICI Bank, one of the largest banks in India, addressing the financing needs of smallholder farmers. While working at ICICI Bank, they witnessed first-hand the storage and financing challenges faced by the smallholder farmers that lead to USD 13 billion of post-harvest losses in India every year. There is a lack of access to high quality warehouses closer to smallholder farmers. This is usually why farmers consider selling the output at the earliest possible chance. Also, by the time the harvest is completed, farmers are usually in a cash crunch situation to support the investments for the next crop cycle. Given the limited access to financing for smallholder farmers, their situation forces them to accept prices available immediately post-harvest, which are usually the lowest, due to high supply. Most times, farmers incur heavy transport costs to carry goods to the nearest market and are often at the mercy of traders who leverage their plight resulting in lower payouts to farmers.

With the objective of helping farmers across the country, Prasanna and Anand set up Arya to offer high quality warehousing facilities closer to farmer locations and improve access to finance. Arya offers loans to farmers against the goods stocked in their warehouses. This allows farmers to tide over the challenges of season end cash flow. It also enables them to hold the produce and later sell it, after the supply glut from the harvest season has subsided. This results in prices that are higher by as much as 20–30 per cent. Arya has also launched a digital marketplace which helps farmers get the best price for their produce by reducing the middlemen in the sales process. Stored commodities are converted to electronic balances that can be offered as loan securities, or can be digitally transferred to other parties, thus making the entire sales process a frictionless one.

Quona invested about USD 10 million in Arya in 2020 as they felt that using technology to improve access to financial services for farmers could play a huge role in improving efficiency and transparency in post-value harvest chain resulting in higher incomes for farmers. Since then, Quona worked closely with Arya to hire the right people and develop its digital and financing capabilities while assisting it in improving governance and compliance and building strategic partnerships. Over time, Arya has evolved into one of the leading agritech companies in India and received interest from several investors raising USD 60 million in 2022[8] and USD 29 million in 2024.[9]

Portfolio Allocation Strategy

As the fund sizes increased, the portfolio allocation strategy also changed. In Fund I, Quona made twenty investments, twenty-five in Fund II and twenty-eight in Fund III. Usually, they have twenty-five to thirty investments in a fund. As fund size increased, the initial investment size has grown as well. Usually, the first cheque is about USD 3–6 million and over the life of the company, they might invest two to three times of that amount. In Fund III, Quona has been a little flexible on the investment size—they have made a few sub-million investments. Over Fund II and Fund III, Quona has increased its focus on pre-Series A and Series A investments. In Fund I, 15 per cent of the funds were deployed in Series B, while in Fund III it is less than 15 per cent.

Quona's portfolio companies have been able to create a massive reach within a short period in terms of the number of SMEs and the number of consumers addressed by them. Several of these companies are recognized as market leaders in their respective countries, such as Creditas, the largest secured asset fintech lender in Brazil; Klar, the most well-known digital bank in Mexico; KoinWorks, the largest SME digital lender in Indonesia; Sunday, the largest insurtech in Thailand and Shivalik, the first bank Quona invested in—one of the very few small finance banks in India that did not originate from a microfinance background. A lot of these companies are truly market leaders and are well recognized today. At the same time, they also have an invention portfolio. As Ganesh explains, 'Some things work out some things don't. But because of our domain expertise and our conservative DNA the downsides have been limited. Compared to typical venture funds, where loss ratios could be 25 or 30%, our loss ratios are much lower - sub 10%.'[10]

Exits

Quona has exited eight investments till date. As the portfolio matures, their team invests significant effort in driving exits. According to Ganesh, the exit outlook has improved significantly since they started, 'Whether from an IPO perspective or from the point of view of large regional players wanting to consolidate or global players wanting to enter some of our markets and looking for a leg up from that, the exit options have opened up significantly. Even some of the new entrants in some markets like the PhonePes or Xendits of the world are looking to consolidate.'[11]

Quona believes that the star companies in their portfolio usually end up carrying forward the baton of impact even after they exit. This is because incoming investors come with the intent of scaling the established business model with proven unit economics. In Ganesh's words, 'If the companies are not doing well and they're trying to find a good home, it almost doesn't matter because they have not anyway scaled up to achieve the impact that they were hoping to. But for successful and scaled up companies, as long as the unit economics makes sense the acquirers are interested because of the success, and they are not looking to inherit and then change it. So, if the company is impactful, and scaled up enough, the exit naturally becomes responsible because the buyer is not paying up to destroy the business. So, with success, responsible exit becomes easier as we expect the mission to be carried forward.'[12]

Impact Measurement

During this entire journey, Quona has stayed true to its mission of transforming the financial services industry to make it more inclusive and more impactful while generating attractive returns for its investors. Quona assesses the impact of its investments throughout their life cycle, by using a simple three dimensional framework.

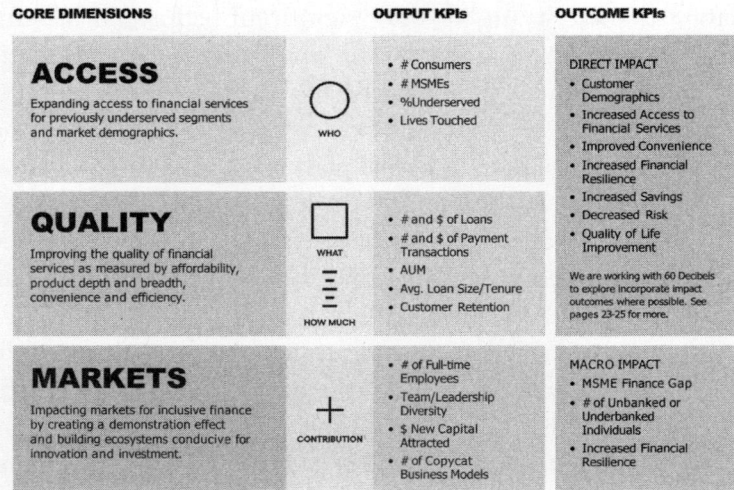

Figure 17: Quona's 3-dimesional framework for impact measurement

Source: Quona Capital 2023 Impact Report, Quona Capital, May 2024, https://quona.com/wp-content/uploads/2024/05/Quona-Capital-2023-Impact-Report.pdf, p. 18.

An impact scorecard is prepared for each investment which looks as follows:

At the end of 2023, Quona had a total AUM of USD 770 million and sixty-eight active portfolio companies. Its portfolio companies had collectively raised USD 4.8 billion in equity. Till date, Quona has reached 160.9 million lives of which 79 per cent were underserved and served 29.6 million retail customers of which 87 per cent were underserved. It also served 8.3 million MSMEs of which 77 per cent were underserved. Quona's portfolio companies have created 22,900 jobs. As per Quona's assessment, 70 per cent of their portfolio companies were benefitting stakeholders on a scale while 8 per cent of the companies were contributing to solutions.

IMPACT POTENTIAL SCORECARD						
Company Name:			**Quona Contribution Thesis:**			
Impact Thesis:						
Title		Category	Considerations	Current Rating	Potential Rating (5 Years)	Rationale
Direct Impact	ACCESS (Who)	Focus on underserved	How underserved is the target segment?	(H/M/L)		
		Scale	How underserved is the target segment?	(H/M/L)		
	QUALITY (How Much; What)	Product breadth	How comprehensively is the company serving the target customer?	(1-4)		
		Convenience/ experience	How convenient, accessible and understandable are the company's products/services vs. alternatives?	(1-4)		
		Affordability	How affordable are the products/services relative to alternatives?	(1-4)		
Indirect Impact	MARKETS (Contribution)	Ecosystem impact	How much of an impact will the company have on a broader market in terms of building enabling ecosystems conducive for innovation and investment?	(H/M/L)		
		Capital crowded in	What level of capital do we expect the company to attract to the region?	(H/M/L)		
		Inclusivity	How diverse is the leadership of the company?	(H/M/L)		
Client Protection (Risk)			What is the level of risk that the company is not fully aligned with the Client Protection Standards?	(H/M/L)		
Impact Milestones			Describe milestones/progress the company should make to be considered an impact "success" at the time of exit.			

Figure 18: Sample impact scorecard

Source: Quona Capital 2023 Impact Report, Quona Capital, May 2024, https://quona.com/wp-content/uploads/2024/05/Quona–Capital–2023-Impact-Report.pdf, p.19.

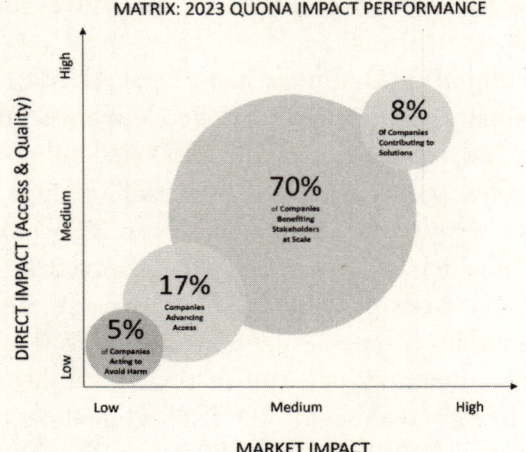

Figure 19: Summary of Quona's impact performance—2023

Source: Quona Capital 2023 Impact Report, Quona Capital, May 2024, https://quona.com/wp-content/uploads/2024/05/Quona-Capital-2023-Impact-Report.pdf, p.21.

In January 2024, Quona completed an audit process by BlueMark, an independent impact verification provider. Quona was rated Advanced on seven out of eight operating principles for impact management, scoring in the top quartile of BlueMark's broad dataset for these principles.

OPERATING PRINCIPLES FOR IMPACT MANAGEMENT	QUONA	BLUEMARK MEDIANS
1. Define strategic impact objective(s), consistent with the investment strategy	Advanced	Advanced
2. Manage strategic impact on a portfolio basis	Advanced	High
3. Establish the Manager's contribution to the achievement of impact	Advanced	High
4. Assess the expected impact of each investment, based on a systematic approach	Advanced	High
5. Assess, address, monitor, and manage potential negative impacts of each investment	Advanced	High
6. Monitor the progress of each investment in achieving impact expectations and respond appropriately	Advanced	High
7. Conduct exits considering the effect on sustained impact	Moderate	Moderate
8. Review, document, and improve decisions and processes based on the achievement of impact and lessons learned	Advanced	Moderate

Figure 20: Assessment of Quona's performance on operating principles for impact management

Source: Quona Capital 2023 Impact Report, Quona Capital, May 2024, https://quona.com/wp-content/uploads/2024/05/Quona-Capital-2023-Impact-Report.pdf, p.17.

For a firm which has been around for only a decade, these are impressive achievements. As their investments continue to scale, Ganesh and the team at Quona look forward to their portfolio creating positive societal impact across sectors including climate, food & agri, healthcare and education by using fintech as a tool.

12

Sustainable Development Capital LLP: Energy Efficiency Is Core to Achieving Net Zero

Jonathan Maxwell, the founder of SDCL, was a student of modern history at the University of Oxford, but even then, he had an interest in resources and the environment. After he graduated in 1995, Jonathan entered the world of investment banking. In 2002, he joined the investment banking division of HSBC. After a couple of years working in the investment bank, he had the chance to work in the infrastructure and real estate investment arm of the bank. HSBC was a pioneer of 'social' infrastructure. The concept of investing in essential services, such as healthcare and education, without which society would not function was incredibly appealing to Jonathan.

A large part of his work involved Public Private Partnership (PPP) projects. He was fascinated by the fact that even though most of the projects or companies in the social infrastructure space were not profit centers, there was a commercially sustainable way to design, finance, build and operate projects by leveraging capital markets. The experience taught Jonathan that, though PPP projects garner their fair share of criticism, the ones that actually flourish are those where both the financial and construction risks are taken by private parties. He was excited at the prospect of enabling popular access to crucial services, at prices that offered significant value for money. In hindsight, he recalls, his exposure to the capital markets before he began to work in investment proved to be valuable. This experience was extremely handy when he worked on listing HSBC's infrastructure portfolio in 2006. That listing created good returns for investors, enabling them to raise more capital.

In 2006, Jonathan travelled to China to help with raising a real assets fund. It was a successful fund raiser, but for Jonathan, it was an eye-opener, to understand just what was possible in the space of environmental infrastructure. It helped him visualize how right policies could stimulate improvements in efficiency. It would become, in later years, one of the main pillars of SDCL. Impressed by China's medium and five-year plans on energy productivity, Jonathan brought his new perspectives back to the United Kingdom, where, at the time, he was also working with the British government and was particularly involved with the United Kingdom-China Sustainable Development dialogue. Jonathan then focused on getting HSBC to start a fund to invest in 'environmental infrastructure', including energy efficiency. He felt that the business models across various infrastructure sectors including clean and renewable energy could evolve well, particularly if they were well supported by the financial models necessary to scale them up. While these focused on addressing the supply part, he felt that there was a massive opportunity in addressing the demand side through improving energy efficiency. Jonathan never stopped being fascinated by the potential of energy efficiency. In fact, it became the subject of his book, *The EDGE: How Competition for Resources Is Pushing the World & Its Climate to the Brink and What We Can Do About It*. The book connects the most important geopolitical events of recent times including the Ukraine war, with current and potential energy challenges and the effect these events have on economies globally. Released to acclaim in 2023, the book tackles pressing concerns for the modern investor.

The problem with global events, Jonathan argues, is that they are often caused by the same problem: competition for coveted and not very plentiful resources. Every society, organization, business, household and individual must put efficiency first— not just to save money and improve their carbon footprint and resilience, but to mitigate and avoid both conflict and climate change. The goal is to help investors and economies across the world transition towards a sustainable economy in modern times. Jonathan captures the essence of energy efficiency in his book in very simple terms. For instance, he states that of the 50 Gt of carbon emitted each year, 40 Gt is energy related, 30 Gt is in buildings, industry and transport and at least 20 Gt is wasted. According to Jonathan, this wasted energy is the largest and cheapest source of greenhouse emissions reductions, as well as productivity and energy security. The World Economic Forum (WEF) estimates that around 70 per cent of energy is lost before it gets to the point of end use. Energy is lost at various stages. There are losses in generation. In 2019 only 45 per cent of the natural gas consumed for electricity generation was turned into electricity in the USA. The balance is lost as heat. Some waste heat from electricity generation can be recycled. However, a large amount of savings can be seen in transmission, if electricity is generated closer to where it is needed. Another large area is energy losses at the point of use due to inefficient appliances. The classic example is the LED lamp, which can reduce energy consumed by a conventional light by 60–90 per cent for the same quality of light, while lasting for 10–15 years. According to Jonathan, in theory, energy efficiency involves using less energy to achieve the same level of output. However, in practice, energy efficiency is achieved by energy saved in generating, supplying, distributing or using energy.

The four ways of measuring energy

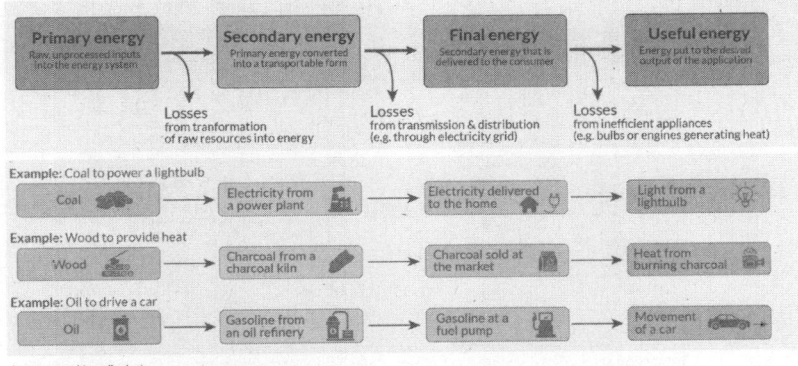

Icon source: Noun Project.
OurWorldinData.org – Research and data to make progress against the world's largest problems.   Licensed under CC-BY by the author Hannah Ritchie.

Figure 21: 70 per cent of energy is lost in converting energy from its primary form to useful form

Source: 'Energy Definitions', Our World in Data, https://ourworldindata. org/energy-definitions.

Considering social, economic and environmental benefit, the Copenhagen Consensus think tank estimates a return on investment of USD 3 for every USD 1 invested in doubling energy efficiency, compared with USD 0.8 for every USD 1 invested in doubling renewable energy. The United Nations Environment Programme's 'minimum ambition' model points to potential for annual savings by 2040 equivalent to 480 power stations, or 970 million tonnes of carbon dioxide. McKinsey's marginal abatement costs curves, which have been published since 2007, have always placed energy efficiency at the lowest end of the curve, which implies that energy efficiency can have the highest impact at the lowest cost.

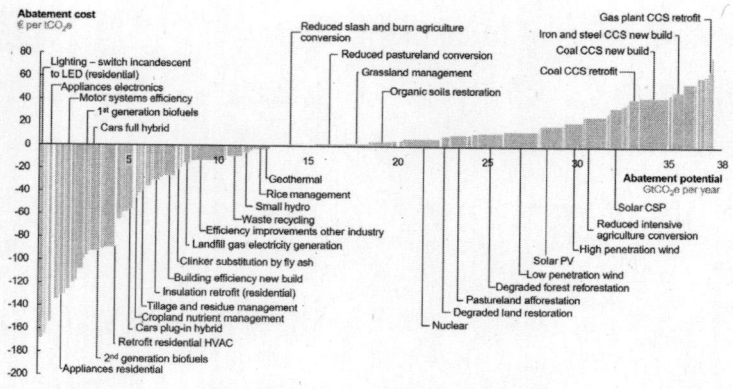

Figure 22: Global greenhouse gases abatement cost curve beyond BAU[1]

Source: Exhibit 6, Page 8, Impact of the Financial Crisis on Carbon Economics Version 2.1, McKinsey & Company.

From where Jonathan stood, he was finally at a place where he could use his understanding of the world of business and finance and his interest in the field to move money into the environmental infrastructure sector. Beyond the maturing renewable energy project sectors, he was convinced that there was an opportunity to fast-track net zero by reducing the amount of energy being used.

Buoyed by the idea, he decided to set up Sustainable Development Capital LLP (SDCL) in 2007, at the age of thirty-three, to focus on environmental infrastructure with a focus on energy efficiency. Jonathan's exit from HSBC served as a catalyst for change, and his new firm was hired immediately by the bank to help design and deliver the strategy of environmental infrastructure. SDCL helped them design and raised a fund focused on renewable energy called the HSBC environmental infrastructure fund. SDCL also worked for other clients, such as the IFC asset management company, which is part of the World Bank, and helped them design a new fund called IFC Catalyst Fund to bring capital into environmental infrastructure and emerging markets. Jonathan also worked on an initiative driven by Prince Charles (now King Charles III) to set up a fund with the objective of bringing capital to emerging markets to address climate change. This involved working with top eight pension funds in UK, Department for International Development (DFID), World Economic Forum (WEF), Asian Development Bank (ADB) and International Finance Corporation (IFC). Several of these development finance institutions (DFIs) appreciated what SDCL did. Notable among them was European Investment Bank (EIB), who had verbally committed to support SDCL if they ever launched a fund focused on energy efficiency.

In 2010, a conservative-liberal coalition government formed in England. Led by David Cameron, this government pledged to be the 'greenest government ever'. Jonathan had come across some of the manifesto's ideas before, including the concept of a 'Green Investment Bank'. The first he had heard of it was when he worked on the UK China Sustainable Development Dialogue with the Government on the Dongtan project in China. Now, Cameron's government had it as a flagship project, the core focus of which would be offshore wind. That made sense to Jonathan. After all, the UK was home to 25 per cent of Europe's offshore wind generation resource and this offered clean energy at scale. He kept an eye on the progress of this initiative, even as SDCL started consulting, that same year, on project development with large multinational companies. Some of these new clients included the world's largest retailers and global brands that were looking to reduce carbon in their supply chains (what is now referred to as 'Scope 3' emissions) because this was where some 90 per cent of the carbon impact of their products took place. SDCL had a multidisciplinary team that collaborated with factories supplying these major brands to design energy efficiency projects. The feasibility studies were initially funded by the not-for-profit Environmental Defense Fund, which it did partly in support of US brands that were members. This involved working on factory floors and figuring out new technologies in areas such as lighting, heating, ventilation, cooling and building management that could reduce energy consumption. However, those factories were not keen on sharing information as they felt that it could be used to squeeze their margins. As a result, brands could place objectives and targets on suppliers but could not enforce them. In the process, Jonathan and his team gained valuable insights, strengthening his resolve that these problems could be solved. But essentially, they gained an answer to a crucial question: Why wasn't energy efficiency happening? Because, as SDCL realized, there were no savings and productivity gains to capture, because of a lack of project development and investment.[2]

That year, the United Nations Climate Change Conference was held in Cancun, Mexico (the Conference of the Parties, or COP16). It was the place to be if you wanted to meet new investors. A few days before the Conference (COP16), Jonathan booked the cheapest economy ticket he could find. Unaccredited, he flew out to Mexico and began to set up meetings and networking dinners. But what really changed the game for him and for SDCL was a quiet conversation during drinks on the balcony with the head of the European Investment Bank's (EIB) climate finance division. Jonathan's pitch was crisp and clear: he wanted to create the first institutional energy efficiency fund. He got a positive response from EIB, but they will not be able to support the fund by themselves.

Around the same time, the consultancy firm McKinsey approached SDCL to partner on their bid for a mandate to advise the UK Treasury on the formation of Green Investment Bank. Again, these were people who had been in Cancun, had heard Jonathan speak and had liked what they heard. This was an institution being planned by the Government to support green energy projects. SDCL joined the consortium with McKinsey and Vivid Economics (which was later acquired by McKinsey). The consortium advised on the financing structure of the project. The structure was simple—to structure project companies to enter into agreements with clients to provide energy as a service while sub-contracting construction and operation to third parties that could execute them. Once the Green Investment Bank was formed, the Government needed managers to implement the plan. SDCL pitched for addressing energy efficiency. Through it all, Jonathan was fully aware that once the project began moving forward, SDCL would have to change its business model. This would imply a change in structure, people and capital base.

In 2011, Jonathan ended up in the lift with a hotel owner while attending a conference in Monaco. During the brief ride, Jonathan told the owner that he could find 30 per cent energy savings in his properties. This, he said, was over and above the fact that the hotel in question had won prestigious Green Tourism awards, and the owner himself believed that his buildings were energy efficient. The hotel owner was intrigued. He made Jonathan a bet: if that promised 30 per cent could be found, he would invest with SDCL to begin driving similar projects that were focused on energy efficiency. That was the start of private projects for SDCL. The company used that money to drive several such projects in hotels and hospitals across London. One thing Jonathan learned from this experience was that SDCL needed to give enough space to building owners to allow them to communicate their issues honestly, through their engineers and data that was being collected every day. In each of these prospective projects, SDCL continued to find large savings.

Later in 2012, SDCL launched the first institutional energy efficiency fund in the UK with government backing. Green Investment Bank, set up by the UK Government, committed GBP 50 million to the energy efficiency fund, which would be unlocked if SDCL could find another GBP 50 million in matched funding. So, Jonathan reached out to all institutions, such as the European Investment Bank, which had shown interest in partnering on a fund. It still took SDCL eighteen months to raise funds. In 2014, SDCL closed the energy efficiency fund, called the UK Energy Efficiency Investments Fund, with GBP 104.1 million. This fund invested in unique projects, including LED lighting for commercial buildings, HVAC systems, building management systems and controls for hospitals and commercial spaces, variable speed drives for warehouses and agriculture, and innovative cooling solutions for data centers. It also invested in cleaner and more efficient energy supply, including solar, recycled waste gases and sustainably sourced biomass, bringing energy directly to the point of use. The fund also invested in distribution projects, electric vehicle charging infrastructure and in the green transport fuel sector. This work led to opening of doors in other places, including conversations with governments in Singapore and Ireland to replicate this model and establish funds.

In Jonathan's opinion, a decided bonus for the company is that SDCL's clients do not view it as a fund but as someone who can help solve their energy problems. SDCL works with them to design a solution that not only improves energy efficiency and reduces carbon footprint but also improves reliability and offers energy security. The company makes its returns from the energy savings delivered. In 2015, when Citibank approached SDCL to address the carbon footprint and cost associated with the energy for their data center, SDCL built an energy center directly on the same site as the data center. The project provided all the cooling and most of the energy for the data center. After building this in London, the project was replicated for Citibank in New York as well. SDCL continues to use similar techniques to decarbonize large data centers. There have been significant innovations in energy efficiency for data centers. These facilities consume 1–2 per cent of a nation's electricity. In fact, energy is so important to data centers that they are measured in Megawatts (MW), not square feet. They use energy to power the server racks and to cool the rooms that they occupy. Liquid cooling solutions that cool the racks rather than the room have a significant impact on both space requirement and energy efficiency. They are now being rolled out on a commercial scale.

One of the most powerful yet simple projects implemented by SDCL was the improvement of the energy efficiency for Santander's offices throughout the United Kingdom in 2015. It involved the replacement of 90,000 lights with LED lights, across more than 800 buildings. It also involved the installation of efficient heating, ventilation, air conditioning and controls. It took around nine months to design and plan this project. The project reduced related energy demand by about 50 per cent, which in turn resulted in lower costs and improvement in infrastructure for Santander. Jonathan states that simple projects like this can actually deliver massive efficiency and savings. For instance, if implemented in hospitals across the UK's National Health Service (NHS) system, a project like this could deliver gains of as much as a billion pounds over a decade, while costing GBP 350–400 million. As a result, it can be easily financed from savings alone.

Investing in similar projects, SDCL took four years to invest its entire capital. By 2018, most of the projects they invested in had already started operating. Once operational, these assets performed like defined yield infrastructure projects with fixed cash flows. Leveraging his experience of working for the first IPO of infrastructure projects during his investment banking days, Jonathan decided to launch an IPO for the fund on the London Stock Exchange (LSE). Despite December 2018 being the worst on the London Stock Exchange since 1930, SDCL successfully attracted investors and went public that month. This also helped Jonathan to fulfill his exit obligations to the fund's investors. The fund had a life of ten years, and the listing provided an opportunity for investors to exit earlier if needed.

The IPO opened up an opportunity for SDCL to raise more capital from the public markets. Over the next four years, SDCL raised another billion pounds for the fund, through a series of ten new equity offerings. The funds were used to invest in new energy efficiency projects. Meanwhile, SDCL launched a special purpose acquisition company to facilitate the public listing of a profitable private company or a division of an existing industrial or utility group. It was called SDCL EDGE. EDGE stands for Efficient & Decentralized Generation of Energy. By the time it listed in October 2021, SDCL had accumulated nearly USD 2 billion worth of investment capital dedicated to energy efficiency in less than a decade. In 2023, SDCL launched and closed another Euro 650 million private fund named Green Energy Solutions Fund, providing Jonathan and his team with more firepower to reduce greenhouse emissions by solving for efficiency. All this while generating good returns for investors, taking the overall assets under management to more than USD 2.5 billion.

Driven by efforts from firms such as SDCL, energy efficiency has continued to gain momentum. In 2019, UK Parliament's Business, Energy and Industrial Strategy Committee published a report titled 'Energy Efficiency: Building Towards Net Zero', which stated that 'the widespread deployment of energy efficiency measures across the UK's buildings will be a key pillar of any credible strategy to meet net zero greenhouse gas emissions by 2025, to tackle fuel poverty and cut energy bills.' The report also estimated that reducing total energy use by 25 per cent by 2035 would result in average energy savings for consumers of roughly GBP 270 per household per year, while sustaining between 66,000 and 86,000 new jobs annually across all regions in the country.

Similarly, the 'energy efficiency first principle' has become one of the pillars of the European Union's policies to help it meet its climate objectives as well as to reduce dependence on fossil fuels. The European Union aims to treat energy efficiency as a source of energy in its own right. In 2020, the European Commission announced a 'Renovation Wave', which aims to double the rate of renovation for energy efficiency from 1 per cent of buildings per annum to 2 per cent per annum by 2030, involving some 35 million buildings in the 2020s. This is expected to reduce building greenhouse gas emissions by 60 per cent, final energy consumption by 14 per cent and energy consumption for heating and cooling by 18 per cent as compared to 2015. In June 2022, Fatih Birol, the executive director of International Energy Agency (IEA), spoke at the IEA's 7th Annual Global Conference on Energy Efficiency hosted in Sonderborg, Denmark. In the speech, Birol stated that doubling the current global rate of energy intensity improvement to 4 per cent a year, compared to today's policies, would save energy equivalent to the current annual energy consumption of China. This would result in savings of 30 million barrels of oil per day, triple Russia's production of 2021 and cut fossil gas use by four times the European Union's imports from Russia. According to IEA's Net Zero by 2050 Pathway, without fundamental consumption changes that include a push towards maximizing energy efficiency, the final energy consumption in 2050 could be 90 per cent above what is required to achieve the net zero pathway. In fact, according to IEA's Sustainable Development Scenario, energy efficiency represents more than 40 per cent of the emissions abatement needed by 2040.

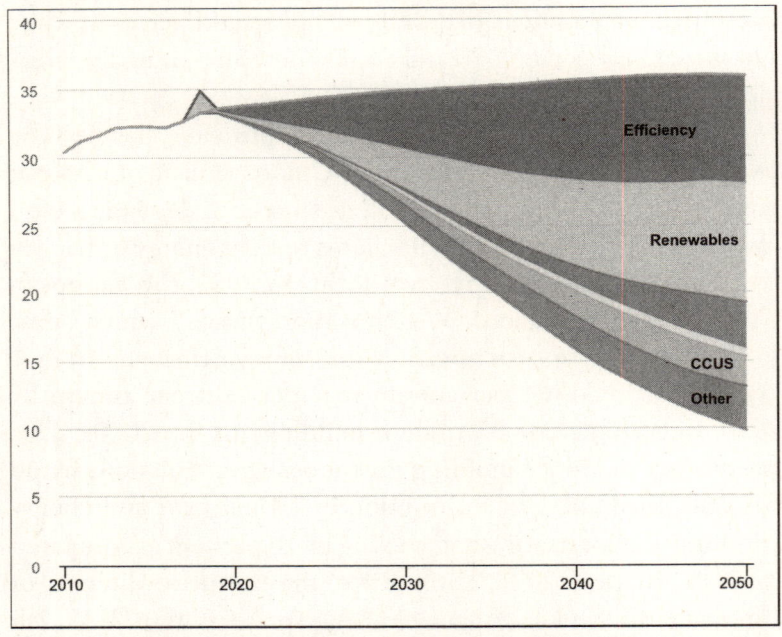

Figure 23: Energy efficiency represents >40 per cent of the emissions abatement needed by 2040

Source: CO$_2$ Emissions Reductions by Measure in the Sustainable Development Scenario Relative to the Stated Policies Scenario (2010–2050), International Energy Agency (IEA), https://www.iea.org/data-and-statistics/charts/co2-emissions-reductions-by-measure-in-the-sustainable-development-scenario-relative-to-the-stated-policies-scenario-2010-2050.

Given the importance of energy efficiency and being one of the few investors globally solving for this, SDCL has continued to receive significant interest from investors. In June 2024, General

Atlantic, one of the leading private equity investors globally, announced an investment of USD 50 million in SDCL to acquire 24.9 per cent stake through its BeyondNetZero fund.

Today, the world faces massive challenges—across climate and economies. Rising prices, a global push to lower carbon emissions and regional conflicts—like Russia's invasion of Ukraine or the ongoing crisis in the Middle East—are pushing the world towards a point of no return. Now, more than ever, impact investment is the need of the hour. For SDCL, as Jonathan himself puts it, the next stage of their journey is just beginning.

13

Verdane: Decarbonization and Digitalization with Sustainability at the Core

Verdane invests in companies that drive and benefit from two structural megatrends: digitalization and decarbonization, with the belief that these spaces will grow faster than the economy at large. Verdane has specifically focused on areas where technology plays a key role as a catalyst in reshaping industries, creating new markets and challenging incumbent business models. Today, Verdane manages more than 8 billion Euros and has made over 200 investments since 2003. It is the first private equity firm to neutralize all residual emissions with permanent carbon removals. At the same time, it has delivered top quartile returns across most of its funds and ranks twelfth among the 106 growth funds across the globe rated by HEC Paris.[1] It has been named the Best European PE Growth Fund all the years between 2019 and 2023 and the Best European mid-market PE fund in 2022. However, this did not happen overnight. It took Bjarne Kveim Lie, the founder of Verdane, and his team almost two decades to build Verdane as one of the most prominent investors.

Bjarne Kveim Lie worked as a naval officer and a historian before he graduated with an MBA from Harvard Business

School in 1999 as a Baker Scholar, an award given to the top 5 per cent of the class. From Harvard, he was recruited by McKinsey and posted to their London office. He had hardly spent five months there before the entrepreneurial bug bit him. He co-founded Paper X, a B2B marketplace, similar to Alibaba in China and Indiamart in India, that allowed businesses to find other businesses that could either supply inputs or purchase their products. Paper X raised 15 million Euros in Series A, which was one of the largest Series A fundraises in Europe at that time, from Apax and Insight Partners. Bjarne was the COO of the firm. The firm scaled to seventy people quickly, but the start-up eventually failed and within seventeen months after starting the firm was shut down. Bjarne considers this failure one of the formative moments in his career. He feels that in hindsight it was one of the best things to happen to him because he fell flat, and it got the ego knocked out of him.

In May 2001, Bjarne joined Four Seasons Ventures, which was one of the two venture capital firms in Oslo, Norway, at the time and focused on early-stage technology investments. He realized very quickly that the fund was subscale and as a result needed to reinvent itself. In 2003, they got an opportunity to acquire a USD 120 million fund from SND Invest, a Norwegian government-backed fund focused on venture capital and private equity. This allowed them the opportunity to make larger investments at a later stage and from then on the firm scaled rapidly raising funds at regular intervals.

As the growth stage funds gained traction, they spun out of Four Seasons and named the new firm Verdane, after the Norse[2] goddess of destiny—Verdandi.[3] Verdane also named its funds after Goddesses—Freya and Idun—and the main collection of Norse mythology (Edda). The growth fund was named Freya after the goddess of love and beauty. The fund that acquired a portfolio of ownership positions from SND invest was named Freya IV since they had three funds at Four Seasons. Since then, they continued to raise similar sized funds of around USD 100–200 million in 2005, 2007 and 2009. Two things changed from then. Bjarne realizing that there is a need to improve their reach and marketing efforts, invested in people to drive that effort. One of the key hires was Frida Einarson, who is a partner now and drives fundraising and investor relations. In 2009, Frida was working with Jefferies in the private placements team that focused on fundraising for private equity funds and was involved in helping raise Freya VII in 2009. She welcomed the opportunity to go back to Sweden and be involved in a firm with focus on sustainability. Also, the exits from funds raised in 2003 and 2005 started reflecting the great work done by the Verdane team. This attracted more investors and eventually led to an increase in the size of the following funds. Verdane raised Euro 1.1 billion in 2023 for Freya XI.

Fund	Vintage	Size
Freya XI	2023	EUR 1.1 billion (USD 1.2 billion)
Freya X	2018	SEK 6.0 billion (USD 700 million)
Freya IX	2016	SEK 3.1 billion (USD 360 million)
Freya VIII	2013	SEK 2.0 billion (USD 300 million)
Freya VII	2009	SEK 1.5 billion (USD 200 million)
Freya VI	2007	SEK 1.0 billion (USD 150 million)
Freya V	2005	SEK 1.1 billion (USD 150 million)
Freya IV	2003	NOK 0.8 billion (USD 120 million)

Figure 24: Growth funds raised by Verdane

In 2018, Verdane also started a buyout fund[4] so that it can provide capital throughout the lifecycle and capture the full digitalization opportunity set in Northern Europe. The fund series was named Edda, after the main written collection of Norse mythology. Verdane delivered strong performance for buyout funds as well and that led to Verdane raising Euro 1.1 billion for Edda III even in a difficult fundraising environment in 2023.

Fund	Vintage	Size
Edda III	2024	EUR 1.1bn (~USD 1.2 bn)
Edda II	2020	EUR 540m (~USD 600m)
Edda I	2018	SEK 3.1bn (~USD 350m)

Figure 25: Buyout funds raised by Verdane

Focus on Sustainability Eventually Led to Impact Funds

Bjarne and the team at Verdane have always focused on sustainability and impact even when the funds had no impact mandate, as they believed that there is substantial value to be unlocked by focusing on sustainability. According to Frida, this focus on sustainability also stems from the awareness of sustainability in the Nordics. In Bjarne's own words, 'Verdane seeks to prove that there is no contradiction between generating world-class returns for investors and being a force for good in society'. By 2019, Verdane had invested in more than fifteen companies that were leveraging technology to address the United Nations Sustainable Development Goals (SDGs).

Investment	Year	Description
Caretech	2006	Developer of nurse call solutions for elderly and geriatric care
Wireless Maingate	2008	Virtual mobile operator for wireless communication between machines (M2M)
NorSun	2009	Manufacturer of high-performance mono-crystalline silicon ingots and high efficiency wafers for the global solar energy industry
Solopower	2009	Pioneer in high-performance thin film solar materials science and a large-scale manufacturer of flexible ultra-lightweight photovoltaic products that are used in rooftop solar solutions
Scanacon	2012	Supplier of recycling solutions that reduce environmental impact of acid-based surface treatment processes in the stainless steel and special metals industry
CRF Health	2013	Provider of technology solutions for simplifying global clinical trials
Bemz	2014	Custom sewn design covers for IKEA furniture
Eniram	2014	Provider of energy management technology to reduce fuel consumption and emissions of maritime industry
JSB	2016	A global leading supplier of core material made primarily from foam and balsa, which is used as construction enhancement for wings in the wind turbine industry.

Polytech	2016	Offers solutions for wind turbines with the purpose of either protecting the wings or improving their efficiency
Jupiter Bach	2016	Leading supplier of nacelle and spinner covers for the windmill business
The Lingit Group	2017	Edtech company offering literacy and accessibility technology
CareerFoundry	2018	Edtech company offering online courses on technology
Momox	2018	Germany's largest sustainable reuse platform
Conexus	2019	Leading provider of digital learning platforms used by thousands of schools and more than one million students worldwide
Kappa Bioscience	2019	Pioneer and innovator in the production of nutraceutical ingredients—primarily of vitamin K2, which plays a key role in improving heart, bone and immune system health

Figure 26: Verdane's impact investments till 2019

While the focus on sustainability has further increased over the last few years and there was more innovation happening in the area, Verdane felt that the large size of their growth and buyout funds restricted them from investing in small but innovative companies focused on driving sustainability and addressing UN SDGs. As a result, Verdane raised Euro 300 million for a separate impact fund in 2021 and named it Idun, after the Norse goddess of youth, spring and rejuvenation. Verdane made eleven investments from the fund in companies that improve access, affordability and quality of healthcare and education or deliver proven products and services that avoid or eliminate emissions and enhance the circularity of our economies including NORNORM, a high-growth furniture subscription service disrupting the B2B furniture value chain; Scanbio, Europe's leading aquaculture waste management provider; and UrbanVolt, a solar-as-service company enabling improved access to renewable energy.

NORNORM: Making Office Furniture Recyclable and Sustainable

NORNORM is a great example of a company that moves the world towards sustainability and benefits from the trend. It was founded in 2020 by Anders Jepsen, who spent more than fifteen years at IKEA driving its expansion in emerging markets and leading globally the largest business areas within furnishing categories, and Jonas Kjelberg, a reputed tech investor with many successes to his name including as former managing director of Skype before it was sold to Microsoft. It is disrupting the traditional office furnishing process, which generates 57 million tonnes of waste worldwide every year as furniture is often disposed of when moving offices by offering a subscription service for selected high-volume office furniture pieces that are sustainable, affordable and flexible. While the concept sounds simple, it requires significant changes in product design and business processes including logistics and customer service to ensure that products have a long shelf life and can be refurbished, packed and moved around easily without significant cost. It also requires a completely different business approach—thinking like a financing company, as clients pay rent for the lease period instead of buying the furniture.

This circular solution with 'as good as new' furniture increases product lifetimes from an average of seven to up to thirty years. According to NORNORM, its circular model reduces CO2 emissions by up to 70 per cent, compared to the traditional model of buying furniture. This has attracted customers ranging from high-growth scale-ups to large corporates, commercial landlords and co-working spaces. It has built a large customer base across more than fifty cities and fifteen countries,[5] and is a clear market leader in workspace solutions. It was initially backed by Inter IKEA, a group of companies that connects IKEA franchisees with range development and suppliers and aligns with the overall IKEA strategic direction. In 2022, Verdane led a EUR 110 million funding round in NORNORM. Since then, Verdane has worked with NORNORM to accelerate its expansion and strengthen its circular business model. Backed by the support and funding, NORNORM has delivered significant growth, with a revenue increase of 105 per cent from 2022 to 2023 and an average annual growth of 73 per cent from 2022 to 2024. Today, NORNORMs circular ecosystem is furnishing workspaces in seventeen countries and fifty-nine cities, helping businesses reduce CO_2 emissions—cutting up to 70% compared to traditional, linear models—through sustainable office furniture solutions.

Verdane Has Linked Incentives to Impact Objectives

Verdane has linked the carried interest in Idun I to its impact goals and has also developed a framework for measuring the avoided emissions through their portfolio. The framework focuses on five key parameters—conditions and system boundaries, reference scenarios, portfolio company, avoided emissions calculation and investment avoidance intensity and has four key steps for measurement:

1. Convert: To ensure a common unit of measurement, Verdane converts the entity or technology into a standardised functional unit, which is aligned with the financial model. For example, for a renewable energy company, it would be MWh (Mega watt hours) of energy produced.
2. Calculate: Emissions per functional unit are calculated based on the chosen reference scenario and corresponding emission factors.
3. Estimate: Emissions savings realised by the portfolio company over the holding period and for a period afterwards are estimated based on the growth trajectory set out in the underwriting case.
4. Scale: Emissions savings are scaled proportional to Verdane's stake in the company.

Idun I's portfolio companies have helped in avoiding emissions of 3.5 million CO2 equivalent tonnes. While it is too early to discuss the return profile of Idun I's portfolio, the financial performance of the portfolio is strong. Verdane raised 700 million Euros for Idun II, backed by returns from investments focused on sustainability that were made from other funds.

Investment Strategy Inspired by Dr Alban

According to Bjarne, Verdane's investment strategy has some parallel with how Dr Alban—the Swedish rapper who shot to fame with 'It's My Life'—approached his career. Dr Alban chose to complete his dental education while pursuing his pop star career. Bjarne believes that Verdane brings this downside protection element into their investment underwriting. According to Bjarne, Verdane can handle such situations because of their team that focuses on value creation, which has significant operating experience across multiple disciplines.

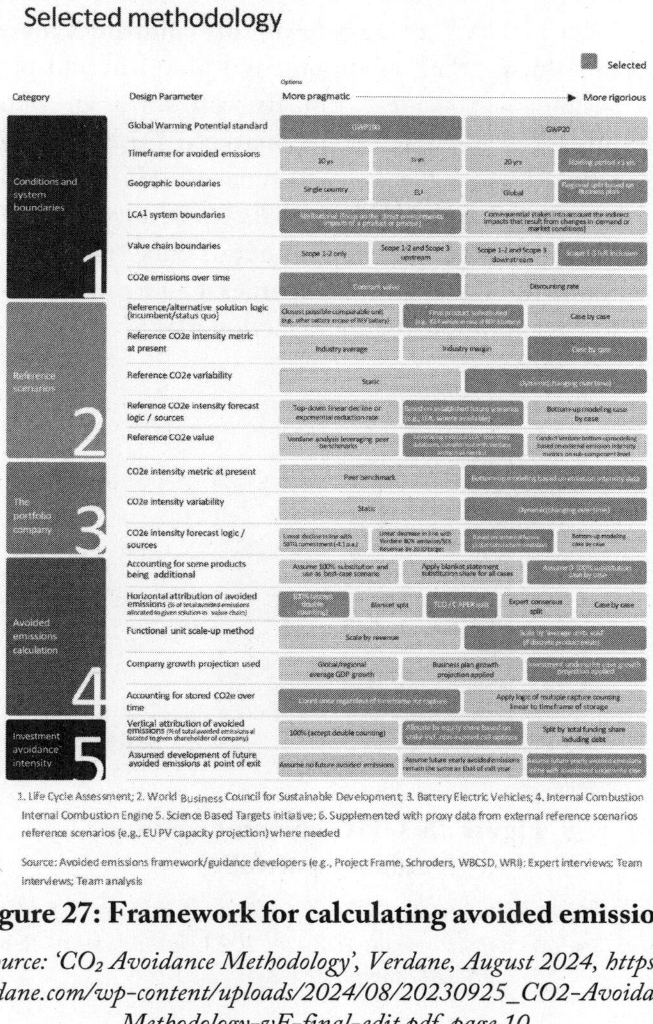

Selected methodology

Figure 27: Framework for calculating avoided emissions

1. Life Cycle Assessment; 2. World Business Council for Sustainable Development; 3. Battery Electric Vehicles; 4. Internal Combustion Internal Combustion Engine 5. Science Based Targets initiative; 6. Supplemented with proxy data from external reference scenarios reference scenarios (e.g., EU PV capacity projection) where needed

Source: Avoided emissions framework/guidance developers (e.g., Project Frame, Schroders, WBCSD, WRI); Expert interviews; Team interviews; Team analysis

Figure 27: Framework for calculating avoided emissions

Source: 'CO$_2$ Avoidance Methodology', Verdane, August 2024, https://verdane.com/wp-content/uploads/2024/08/20230925_CO2-Avoidance-Methodology-vF-final-edit.pdf, page 10.

Three Goals for a Better World

Verdane focuses on three principles to serve as a guiding light for its portfolio companies and itself.

- **Respect the Planet**: Given the unanimous agreement among experts that we must cut global emissions by half by 2030, Verdane believes that companies that excel in reducing their environmental footprint and pioneer sustainable business models will have an outsized impact on their respective markets. Verdane's primary focus thus far has been to reduce GHG emissions in scopes 1, 2 and 3.[6] The initial step involves a thorough assessment of emission sources. This creates a solid foundation for their companies to identify reduction levers and implement a reduction plan.

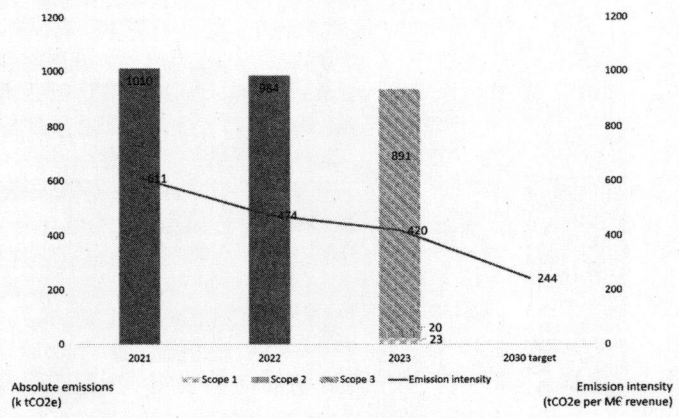

Figure 28: GHG emissions across Verdane's portfolio

Source: '2023 Sustainability Report', Verdane, August 2024, https:// verdane.com/wp-content/uploads/2024/08/2023-Sustainability-Report_ FINAL-compressed-2.pdf, p.31.

Emissions Category	Share of total emissions	Key drivers of emissions	Steps to reduce emissions
Scope 1-2	11 per cent	Natural gas and fuel used in vehicles, electricity consumption, and district heating are the main sources of scope 1 and 2 emissions.	• Switched to 100 per cent renewable energy at production sites in Lithuania and Denmark • Explored solutions to increase renewable energy coverage in China and Poland
Scope 3	89 per cent	Purchased goods and services, including materials for production, are the main sources of scope 3 emissions	• Conducted market screening for more sustainable raw material options for those that account for two-thirds of its scope 3 emissions • Started a dialogue with key suppliers to gain insights into their efforts towards potential reductions and greener materials • Collaborated with a partner to repurpose fiberglass waste, diverting it from incineration

Verdane has set an ambitious goal to reduce portfolio greenhouse gas (GHG) emission intensity by 60 per cent by 2030 vs 2021, which is measured on a year-on-year basis. To achieve these targets, it works with portfolio companies on several aspects that help reduce emissions. For instance, it helped Jupiter Bach, one of its portfolio companies, to create a climate action plan to be carbon neutral for scopes 1 and 2 by 2025 and to set a reduction strategy ahead. Jupiter Bach is a global leader in the wind industry. It designs and manufactures nacelles and spinner covers, which shield and protect key components of wind turbines, with a track record of more than 70,000 wind turbines around the world. The company's vision is to help drive the industry forward by challenging the status quo, lowering wind power's Levelized Cost of Energy (LCoE) and continually raising the bar for collaboration. It has already taken several steps to achieve its targets.

- **Be the Best Place to Work, for everyone:** Securing and maintaining top talent remains a cornerstone of success for technology-enabled and socially conscious companies. Verdane uses Employee Net Promotor score (eNPS) as a benchmark indicator of organizational health. The eNPS is a crucial metric as it enables Verdane to monitor the level of employee engagement across their portfolio. A score above twenty is widely recognised as positive across industries and geographies. The current score of Verdane's portfolio companies is twenty-four. Verdane also believes that a diverse workforce drives creativity and innovation, bringing unique perspectives that lead to better decision-making and solutions. Hence, it measures diversity at the board, management, and company-wide level.

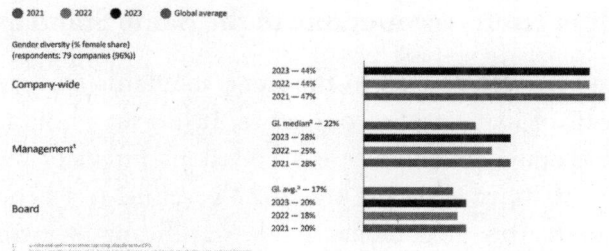

Figure 29: eNPS results from surveys

Source: '2023 Sustainability Report', Verdane, August 2024, https://verdane.com/wp-content/uploads/2024/08/2023-Sustainability-Report_FINAL-compressed-2.pdf, p.35.

- **Create secure and responsible companies:** To ensure companies act responsibly, Verdane ensures codes of conduct outline expectations for employees as well as suppliers at every portfolio company. Verdane's portfolio companies must facilitate whistleblowing and provide protection to anyone who reports incidents. It expects portfolio companies to have these policies and systems in place, regardless of whether they are legally required.

Verdane measures the progress of its portfolio companies towards these goals on a regular basis as shown in the table below.

Figure 30: Snapshot from Verdane's 2023 sustainability report

Source: '2023 Sustainability Report', Verdane, August 2024, https://verdane.com/wp-content/uploads/2024/08/2023-Sustainability-Report_FINAL-compressed-2.pdf, p.9.

Holding Itself Accountable to the Same Standards

Verdane has committed to the same standards and goals that it expects of its portfolio companies. It has set a bold target to reduce scope 3 greenhouse gas emissions intensity by 65 per cent by 2030, considering the 2022 baseline as a benchmark. To achieve this goal, it has made significant investments in digital infrastructure to reduce the need for business travel and secured the 'low hanging' scope 1 and 2 emission reductions by exclusively purchasing renewable power for their offices. To address their inevitable residual footprint, Verdane pledged several years ago to neutralize all residual scope 1–3 greenhouse gas emissions through engineered, permanent carbon removal. This commitment effectively imposes an internal carbon tax exceeding Euro 300/tCO2, a testament to their belief in doing what is right for the planet. Verdane is certified as a B corporation, the most ambitious sustainability accreditation globally. B corporations are businesses that demonstrate the highest standards of social and environmental performance, transparency and accountability.

As an extension of their efforts to identify potential carbon credit providers, Verdane engaged in a discussion with the leading Nordic pulp and paper company Södra with the goal to explore the feasibility of using trees as a carbon sponge, capturing the carbon at the pulp mill and transporting it to the North Sea for storage in depleted and abandoned oil fields. This project named Njord Carbon structured as a joint venture with Södra is at the forefront of developing commercial scale, high-quality permanent carbon removal projects, utilising Bioenergy with Carbon Capture and Storage (BECCS) technology.

Figure 31: Process for using trees as a carbon sponge

*Source: '2023 Sustainability Report', Verdane, August 2024,
https://verdane.com/wp-content/uploads/2024/08/2023-
Sustainability-Report_FINAL-compressed-2.pdf, p.44.*

Verdane also measures its own progress on all the three goals mentioned above as shown in the table below.

Figure 32: Verdane's performance on its three key goals

*Source: '2023 Sustainability Report', Verdane, August 2024,
https://verdane.com/wp-content/uploads/2024/08/2023-
Sustainability-Report_FINAL-compressed-2.pdf, p.10.*

Sustainability Is at the Core of Every Process

At Verdane, sustainability is integrated throughout the investment life cycle from sourcing and closing deals to portfolio management and exit.

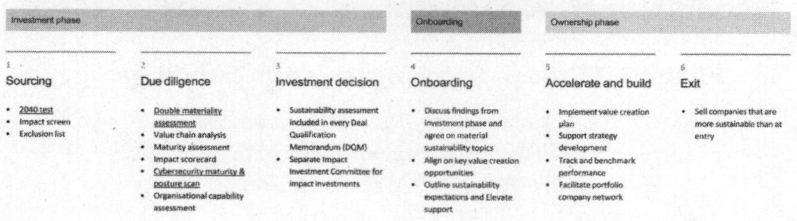

Figure 33: Sustainability is integrated at all stages

Source: '2023 Sustainability Report', Verdane, August 2024, https://verdane.com/wp-content/uploads/2024/08/2023-Sustainability-Report_FINAL-compressed-2.pdf, p.14.

It Starts with Sourcing Companies That Thrive in a Sustainable Economy

Beyond ensuring that their investments avoid the exclusion list and meet the impact criteria (specifically for the decarbonization fund), Verdane invests only in companies with long-term, future-proof business models and sustainable operations—positioning them for success in a more sustainable economy. Verdane calls this the '2040 test'. It is primarily used to determine if the company will thrive in a more sustainable economy. The test explores assumptions about what the world will look like in 2040, such as higher carbon taxes and evolving regulations, with each potential investment screened based on these scenarios. The outcome of the 2040 test for a hypothetical cybersecurity company could look as follows:

Question	Assessment
Would the company succeed if consumers/businesses increasingly integrate sustainability into purchasing decisions? *Customers will avoid purchasing products and services that have a negative sustainability impact*	Strengthens company's position
Would a carbon tax of Euro 200/tCO_2 emitted materially impact profitability? *Carbon will at some point be priced—will that improve or reduce the right to win*	No concern
Would meaningful regulations and/or taxes on other externalities materially impact profitability? *Other negative externalities will increasingly be regulated and, at some point, be priced*	No concern
Are people treated decently in the value chain? *Low risk of human rights violations or corruption across value chain*	No concern
Would the company's customers also pass the 2040 Test? *Very low share of 'sin customers' e.g. gambling, fossil fuels industry, tobacco*	Double Click

● Strengthens company's position ● No concern ● Double click
● Reconsider case

Figure 34: Sample 2040 test

Due Diligence Further Emphasizes Sustainability

Verdane takes six key actions during the due diligence process to evaluate sustainability of its investments.

1. Double materiality assessment: This is used to identify, assess and ultimately choose the ESG topics that are most important for each company. The assessment is based on a long list of ESG topics aligned with the European Sustainability Reporting Standards (ESRS).

   The importance of an ESG topic is determined across two dimensions, impact materiality and financial materiality. Impact materiality refers to a company's actual or potential impacts on people or the planet and financial materiality refers to an ESG topic that affects or may affect financial performance.

   The illustration below is an example of a materiality mapping for a software company operating in the financial services industry.

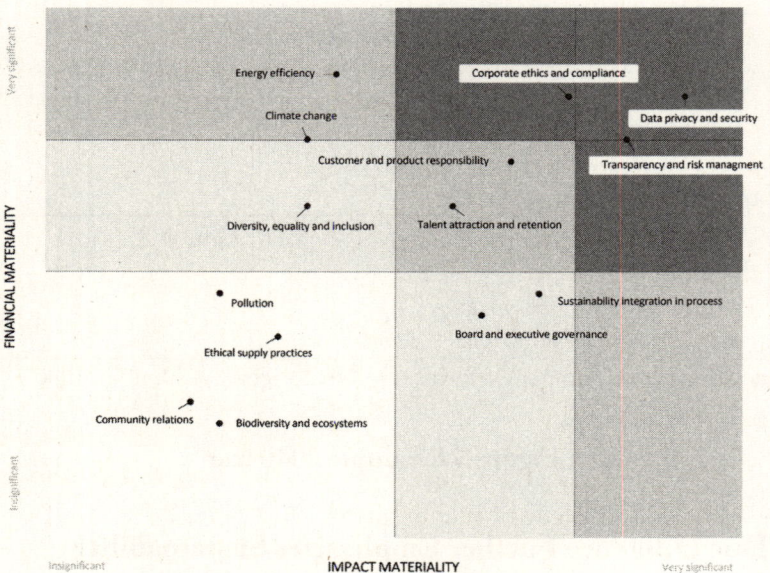

Figure 35: Double materiality assessment

Source: '2023 Sustainability Report', Verdane, August 2024, https://verdane.com/wp-content/uploads/2024/08/2023-Sustainability-Report_FINAL-compressed-2.pdf, p.19.

2. Value chain analysis: The team then evaluates material opportunities and risks for each ESG topic selected. This helps Verdane leverage sustainability as a competitive advantage and identify potential risks and mitigating actions.
3. Maturity assessment: A preliminary evaluation of a company's ESG maturity is conducted, identifying potential improvement areas and opportunities to bolster operations.
4. Impact scorecard: Verdane uses a proprietary impact qualification framework developed in collaboration with Bridgespan Social Impact, a leading social impact consultancy, to underwrite the efficacy of their impact investments. The framework assesses four key dimensions

   a. Intentionality: Management's alignment on prioritizing and growing the positive impact of the business
   b. Additionality: Clear opportunity for Verdane as owners to drive value creation in terms of additional impact and sustainable operations
   c. Total Impact: Clear impact generated by the company's product/service or product/service enables positive impact. The impact is reliably quantifiable and would not have occurred independently
   d. Risk: Limited potential negative impact pathways, clearly outweighed by the positive impact and/or subject can be mitigated

The impact assessment for NORNORM, which offers furniture-as-a-service is as follows:

100%
Intentionality

Develop a long-term sustainable business model that reduces co2 emissions and resource intensity.

67%
Measurability

100% of business from impactful business lines.

89%
Scalability

CO2 avoidance expected to grow by 8x during ownership period.

75%
Risk

Some risks identified but clear mitigation efforts in place (e.g. negative externalities in the furniture supply chain).

Figure 36: Sample impact assessment (NORNORM)

Source: '2023 Sustainability Report', Verdane, August 2024, https://verdane.com/wp-content/uploads/2024/08/2023-Sustainability-Report_FINAL-compressed-2.pdf, p.26.

5. Cybersecurity maturity: The cybersecurity due diligence aims to understand the maturity of the company, identify relevant risks and provide input on how the company can achieve an adequate state within an acceptable timeline and cost. The due diligence includes a cyber security posture scan, which utilizes a cybersecurity platform called Security Scorecard, which offers data-driven assessments of the company's security posture, identifies vulnerabilities and benchmarks performance against industry peers. Based on data, the platform provides predictive insights into the probability of a security breach. For instance, a company with a security rating below 50 ('F') is 13.8 times more likely to be breached compared to one rated 100 ('A'). The illustration below shows an example of a posture scan, and the elements covered.

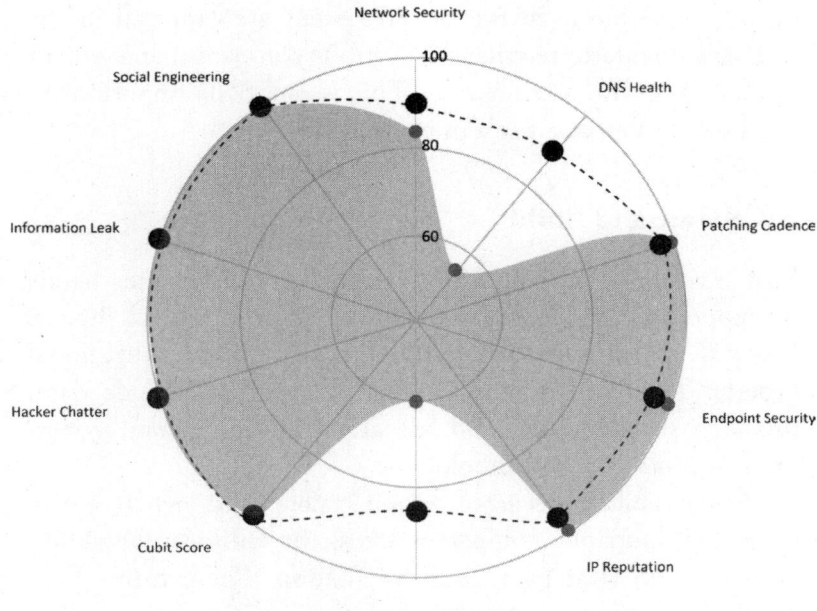

Figure 37: Sample cybersecurity maturity assessment

Source: '2023 Sustainability Report', Verdane, August 2024,
https://verdane.com/wp-content/uploads/2024/08/2023–
Sustainability-Report_FINAL-compressed-2.pdf, p.20.

6. Organizational assessment: The due diligence also
    includes a thorough employee assessment and evaluates
    satisfaction, diversity, inclusion, psychological safety
    and well-being, ensuring that Verdane supports
    companies that respect their people and raise the bar
    post-investment.

Agree on the Path Forward During Onboarding

Post diligence, the investment team discusses findings, align
on key value creation opportunities and agree on sustainability

expectations. Some of the material steps are captured in the legal documentation so that the portfolio company management is aligned on the way forward. This is especially important in cases where Verdane has a minority stake.

Accelerate and Build

Post investing, Verdane offers its portfolio companies hands on support to implement key value creation initiatives though Elevate, an in-house team of more than thirty operational experts. The Elevate team's areas of expertise include data, finance, sustainability and decarbonization, talent, go-to market, product and technology.

Sustainability, decarbonization, talent and cybersecurity teams help portfolio companies across the entire sustainability journey, from strategy to implementation. These teams have developed scalable solutions and frameworks that can be leveraged across the entire portfolio. These tools include standardized strategy blueprints and sustainability software solutions. In 2023, the teams completed around seventy projects and held sparring sessions with more than fifty portfolio companies. These projects and sessions covered a wide range of focus areas, from benchmarking to strategy development.

Exit

Verdane's goal is to ensure that its portfolio companies are more sustainable by the time it exits. This enables Verdane to also benefit financially as it increases the attractiveness of those assets which in turn could lead to more competition for the assets and a better return outcome.

Sustainable World and Returns Go Hand-in-Hand

According to Bjarne, Verdane seeks to prove that there is no contradiction between generating world-class returns for investors and being a force for good in society. This overarching ambition has guided the companies they have invested in, and how they help develop and future-proof those companies during their ownership. Considering the consistent top-quartile performance over two decades and multiple funds, this seems to be a great template for other private equity and venture capital firms to follow.

Epilogue

When I first joined an impact investing firm in 2017, I had the responsibility of investing in healthcare companies that improve access and affordability of healthcare products and services for low- and middle-income people across south and south-east Asia. Initially, I felt that such additional restrictions might result in suboptimal investing outcomes. It took me a while to realize that those restrictions were in fact helping me uncover opportunities in areas that nobody else was focusing on.

Impact Investing Sharpens Focus on Real Value

As investors, we have the fiduciary responsibility to chase returns in line with the promises made to institutions and people who allocate capital to us. One of the hardest things about being a private markets investor is delivering exits. Often there is not enough value accreted to create good exit outcomes in less than three years and anything beyond six years becomes too late. While a three to six-year horizon looks really long term from a public market perspective, only private market investors understand how difficult it is to get those exits. And because exit is such a critical factor, since technically there is no value created without exit, a lot of time is spent to understand whether you are investing in assets which could be target of acquisitions from other large corporations or if a listing of the asset is possible. If one of these two are possible, then there is a good chance you might also attract interest from other private market investors.

This focus on exit eventually leads to private market investors thinking of themselves as slightly longer-term traders—buy now and focus on selling three to five years from now—and as a result they start assigning a lot of value to what the market thinks about the sector and the asset they are investing in. This fosters groupthink, with nearly everyone chasing the same trends, aiming to invest in assets that can be sold within three to five years. In such an approach, a key factor in an asset's saleability is how it is perceived today. Once your judgement is based on others' perception of those assets, you start valuing assets based on how they will be valued by others in future and lend yourself to be subject to 'greater fool theory', i.e. convincing yourself that an asset is attractive to buy because there will be a bigger fool who will buy the assets from you at an even more attractive price or vice versa.

I have seen this kind of group thinking lead to investors chasing the latest hot sectors in the market. A good example of this is the construction sector in India. In the mid to late 2000s, construction became an investor favourite. India was experiencing a boom in construction, and companies such as L&T, riding the wave saw strong investor interest, driving up stock prices. Several brokerage houses were publishing reports talking about the long-term potential in the sector. However, one of the critical challenges with construction sector is that the customer is largely Government—as Transport and Irrigation made up a substantial part of the order book for most of these companies. As a result, there is hardly any differentiation between different companies as they win the new projects based on offering the lowest price during the bidding process.

However, in the late 2000s, the construction sector benefited from a favorable demand-supply scenario, as the Government of India was eager to launch numerous projects. Without any clear moat, the construction sector should have been seen as a commodity sector and should not have attracted interest from long-term investors, especially in private equity. However, a few successes in some of the companies led to investors chasing these assets to such an extent that eventually almost every private equity firm in the market had a construction business in their portfolio and this led to a glut. Most of those investors who were chasing easy deals in the construction sector were stuck with those assets for a long time and could not exit. I have my share of stories about being stuck with a few such assets and learning a painful lesson—just because a company is popular at the moment doesn't mean it's a good business. You should rely on your own assessment of the market, the company's competitive advantages and positioning. And looking back, I could never understand why I thought the construction sector could lend itself to any kind of differentiation.

Another example in recent times was the severe uptick in demand for technology companies post COVID. After the pandemic, most of the stocks worldwide took a beating. However, in a few months, it was clear that the whole world was going digital at an unprecedented rate. As a result, most of the technological start-ups witnessed significant growth in a short period of time which in turn led to significant growth in investor demand. It also helped with that quantitative easing that followed COVID led to more money in the hands of the investors. While I experienced the heydays of 2006–07, when everything was growing, this was way beyond that, especially in the technology sector. I remember getting calls from investment bankers assisting tech companies with fundraising—practically pressuring me to decide on the spot if I wanted an allocation in the round. However, this time, as an impact investor, I was focused on creating real value by investing in products and services that were creating value for the consumers and that helped me stay away from the frenzy. In hindsight, even though I was once bitten and should have been twice shy, I think it would have been slightly harder to stay away from that frenzy if it were not for the focus on real value.

Focus on Real Value Also Reduces Risk

I have believed in the potential of impact investing to help uncover new investment ideas for a while. However, only recently during a conversation with one of the investors did I realize that focusing on real value also helps to minimize the risk. This point is also made by Douglas Hansen-Luke, the founder of Future Planet, when he shared the example of *Pokemon Go*, which has no inherent value and eventually fizzled out. Sectors that create real value such as financial services, healthcare, education and food and agriculture are often associated with low risk. As a result, even if these investments lead to returns similar to those of other sectors they lead to better risk adjusted returns.

As demonstrated by the investors in the book, approaching investing with the objective to create real value, has helped them in outperforming across all the four critical parts of private investing—from origination and assessment to portfolio management and exit.

Origination: Investors know that they are likely to generate good returns when they invest in assets that create value. However, when the north star is generating returns, it is much more likely that you will get persuaded by what other people are doing. On the other hand, if your north star is to invest in assets which will solve real problems and create real value, which in turn will help you generate returns, it helps drown out the sirens alluring you to follow the crowd. As we have seen across several examples, investors presented in this book have been able to make investments in areas often considered unattractive by a wider audience. This is made possible by the fact that they were chasing real value and that eventually led to their strong performance.

Assessment: According to Warren Buffett, to be a successful investor—'You have to figure out where you've got an edge. And you've got to play within your own circle of competence. The size of that circle is not very important; however, knowing its boundaries is vital.' Investors in this book have been able to define their circles very well and because they know what they are looking for, it leads them to avoiding play on the greater fool theory, which is often the case during periods of excess.

Portfolio Management: There have been instances in my past when I have overlooked certain aspects while evaluating portfolio companies, especially when the company is performing well. I have discovered that the chances of that happening are much lower as an impact investor. Even when companies are performing well, impact investors focus on impact metrics and most of these metrics relate to customer experience and hence are lead indicators of business performance. As you have seen, investors in this book have also focused on adding significant value to their portfolio companies.

Exit: Most of the impact investors work towards improving the profile of the company and in the process reduce several risks associated with such enterprises. This improves the attractiveness of the assets and hence leads to not only higher probability of exit but also better return outcomes.

Time to Throw the Kitchen Sink at SDGs

In 2010, when Nadal was preparing for the US Open, he was keen to win the only grand slam missing from his trophy cabinet. He had already won French Open five times, Wimbledon twice and Australian Open once by then. He knew that on the fastest surface across grand slams, his serve, which was slower than many other competitors, was a weak point. He worked with his uncle and coach Tony Nadal to increase the speed of his serve. To achieve that, he started hitting the ball as fast as he could without worrying about whether the serve was legal and landing in the right place. Once he realized that he could hit the ball fast, he then focused on landing it in the right place. He ended up winning the US Open that year.

A similar approach is required to scale impact investing. I am not the only one with the belief that impact investing could lead to better risk adjusted returns. This is a belief being shared by millions and is leading to large amounts of money being invested for impact. As a result, the flows into impact are getting larger. As they get larger, more people are focusing on impact. This has led to some original impact investors questioning the intent of those joining the bandwagon now—are they in for the returns or impact? Some investors are being targeted for being inauthentic in their pursuit of impact and are being labelled as 'Greenwashers' or 'Impactwashers'.

Greenwashing happens when a company makes an environmental or social claim about its actions, aiming to create a sense of environmental impact that is at best misleading and at worst non-existent. The green claim is typically about some form of positive effect on the environment. So, do we focus on greenwashing? Do we assess whether an investor is in it for profit or for the impact?

The right answer in my view is a controversial one and it's likely to win me criticism from most of my colleagues in the impact space

My answer is: 'it doesn't matter'.

What do I mean? either way, impact investment—whether it is being done purely for the returns or for the proper motives—is good for the industry or sector in which it is being made. In today's world, we need to attract as much capital as possible towards impact. It does not matter who is raising the capital as long as it goes to areas that need to be addressed. Given that most investors who raise impact capital would in turn be answerable to those that provided capital, there are sufficient guardrails in place to ensure that they do not sway significantly from the intent. Those wide guardrails should be sufficient at this point in time. We can worry about greenwashing when the industry gets large enough. It's a bit like Nadal, who only introduced new constraints once he knew he could serve fast. For now, there is no reason to judge. Everyone should be focused on only one thing—trying to raise the trillions needed to address SDGs and especially critical challenges such as climate change, inclusion and better health.

Acknowledgements

A project like this doesn't happen without the support of many, and for a working professional, it demands infinitely more. This book would never have seen the light of day without the unwavering support and immense effort of my wife, Roopa. She not only shouldered the additional responsibility of managing our two kids and home entirely on her own but also actively contributed by reviewing, researching and editing the manuscript. As an investment banker, she already understood investments, yet she went a step further and took a course on sustainability to contribute even more meaningfully. She should, in all fairness, be the co-author of this book—this work is as much hers as it is mine—but she chose not to be.

Another person who could have been the co-author is Pritesh Modi, my ex-colleague from LeapFrog Investments and a good friend. We ideated this project together after he published his book *The Year of Doing Nothing* but due to time zone differences and his heavy travel schedule that comes with handling insurance investments globally at DEG, he opted out after initial ideation but has continued to share his thoughts, make introductions and be a guide. To anyone thinking of a trip to get from Singapore to Antarctica while exploring everything in between with just one flight (to cross the Atlantic), I highly recommend his book.

Many thanks to the whole of BlueOrchard for allowing me to embark on this project while being employed with them. It truly shows how supportive BlueOrchard (and its parent Schroders) is of impact even though they don't get any credit in this book for being one of the champions of impact and one of the truest investors who started investing for impact way before the word impact was coined. While there are many people to acknowledge, I would like to specifically thank the senior management and board, including Richard Oldfield, Georg Wunderlin, Peter Fanconi, Philipp Mueller, Marita Teresa Zappia, Michael Wehrle and Matthew Sparkes, as well as my colleagues in Private Equity—Martin Diaz Plata, Felix Hermes and Ernesto Costa—who wholeheartedly supported this. Martin even helped me connect with Michael O'Leary, who wrote the excellent book *Accountable* and was kind enough to share his insights. I am also grateful to my colleagues in Asia— Yvonne, Anushree, Alice and Thibaud—whose exceptional skills ensured we never faltered, even when I did. I want to emphasize that the thoughts in this book are my own, and BlueOrchard is not responsible for any of the material—though they certainly deserve credit for their unwavering support.

My journey in impact would not have started without LeapFrog Investments. I am thankful to Michael Fernandes and Dr Felix Olale for giving me the opportunity to join the healthcare team at LeapFrog. I am deeply indebted to Michael for being a great mentor throughout the entire project. His combination of exceptional intelligence that always finds solutions for every problem and a human touch that empowers people is rare in the corporate world. Naturally, a lot of his ideas have flown into this book. I am extremely grateful to Andy Kuper for setting up LeapFrog and being an incredible champion of impact. I still remember Andy's email accompanying the first quarterly report post my joining at LeapFrog. There were many achievements there including some great exits and new investments but the achievement he was most proud of was how we were solving problems for low and middle-income consumers in emerging markets. He is one of the key pillars of the impact investing industry and was also kind enough to read the book and share his insights to make it better. I would also like to thank my colleagues at LeapFrog including Jasvir, Mark, Pranav, Fernanda, Roshni and Raghu, who helped me frame my own thesis when I first started in impact.

I am deeply grateful to all the investors featured in this book. Their dedication in continuously reviewing and updating the content was invaluable. They stood by me throughout this journey, never once complaining—even when I took far more of their time than initially promised. I hope this book does justice to their efforts, as I consider them true champions of impact.

I would like to extend special thanks to Adrian Li from AC Ventures; Matteo Stefanel, Udayan Goyal, Stephanie Mullard and Ravi Bhatt from Apis Partners; Dave Richards from Capria; Douglas Hansen-Luke and Jessica Hill from Future Planet; Vishal Mehta and Venky Natarajan from Lok Capital; Ganesh Rengaswamy from Quona; Jonathan Maxwell from SDCL; and Frida Einarson and Bjarne Kveim Lie from Verdane.

There were many people who helped me reach out to the right people at these firms including Vijay Advani, ex-chairman of Nuveen and Franklin Templeton, Rajesh Sehgal, my ex-colleague from Franklin Templeton and founder of Equanimity Ventures, Emanuel Citron from SDCL and my ex-colleague Sahib Maker. I am deeply indebted to Saurabh Mukherjea, who helped me build conviction in my research as an analyst and has been a phenomenal mentor during my book-writing journey. I would also like to thank Sugandhi Matta, chief impact officer at ABC Impact, and Rekha Unnithan, global head of private equity impact investing at Nuveen, for their support.

A special shout-out to all my ex-colleagues who helped me frame my investment thesis. I would like to thank Priyank Singhal and Sumeet Budhraja at Edelweiss, Deepa Sankaran, Arun Luharuka and Gaurav Gairola at Darby, Satish Mandhana, Shyam Sundar SG, Gaurav Sharma, Girish Nadkarni, Raja Parthasarathy, Prasad Gadkari, Nithin Kaimal and Vinod Giri at IDFC Private Equity.

I would not have achieved the goal of getting this book published without the encouragement and support of my agent, Kanishka Gupta, who not only guided me on structuring but also connected me with Narayani Basu, a brilliant editor who helped shape and present the content in a way that makes it readable. I am eternally grateful to Radhika Marwah from Penguin for believing in this book and creating a plan that even a newbie like me could follow, and to Sakshi Sharma and Aninda Das for their patience and kindness throughout the editing process. I would also like to thank Vinod Joseph, my ex-colleague, who introduced me to Kaniskha when I reached out to him for advice.

I am grateful for my greatest blessings—my kids, Aurik and Avyaan, who inspire me to do better, my super supportive siblings—Kusum and Dinesh, and my parents, Keshar Dev and Prabha, who invested every penny they could save in our education, hoping I would make a difference.

Notes

Preface

1 'Global e-commerce share of retail sales from 2015 to 2027', *Statista*, 4 December 2024, https://www.statista. com/statistics/534123/e-commerce-share-of-retail-sales-worldwide/

2 'Industry: E-commerce boom in India a matter of concern: Goyal', *Financial Express*, 10 February 2025, https://www. financialexpress.com/business/industry-e-commerce-boom-in-india-a-matter-of-concern-goyal-3589057/

Introduction

1 'Earth Overshoot Day', *Global Footprint Network*, n.d., https://overshoot.footprintnetwork.org/about-earth-overshoot-day/

Part 1: The Playground for H.I.T. Investing

1. The Microfinance Revolution

1 Kaushik Basu, *The Bangladesh Economy: Navigating the Turning Point*, MIT Press, n.d., http://direct.mit.edu/itgg/article-pdf/13/1-2/28/1978760/inov_a_00281.pdf

2   Campbell, 'From Banker to the Poor to Bloodsucker', *TIME Magazine*, 24 June 2024, https://time.com/6991107/muhammad-yunus-trial-sheikh-hasina-bangladesh/

3   Ibid.

4   R. Burgess and R. Pande, 'Do rural banks matter? Evidence from the Indian social banking experiment', *DEDPS Discussion Paper*, No. 40, 2003.

5   Philip Mader, 'Rise and Fall of Microfinance in India: The Andhra Pradesh Crisis in Perspective', *Strategic Change*, Vol. 22, https://pure.mpg.de/rest/items/item_1971501/component/file_1976796/content

6   'The performance of the Integrated Rural Development Program in India—An Assessment', *IDE Discussion Paper*, Available at: https://www.ide.go.jp/library/English/Publish/Periodicals/De/pdf/98_02_01.pdf

7   Mahesh Langa, 'Elaben Bhatt, Gandhian, SEWA Founder & Women's Empowerment Activist Dies', *The Hindu*, 2 November 2022, https://www.thehindu.com/news/national/sewa-founder-ela-bhatt-dies/article66086421.ece

8   Philip Mader, 'Rise and Fall of Microfinance in India: The Andhra Pradesh Crisis in Perspective', *Strategic Change*, Vol. 22, Available online at: https://pure.mpg.de/rest/items/item_1971501/component/file_1976796/content
     Also see, *NABARD*, *Status of Microfinance in India 2011–2012*, National Bank for Agriculture and Rural Development, Micro Credit Innovations Department, Mumbai, http://www.nabard.org/pdf/MF%20book%20-%20full.pdf
     'FAQs: Priority Sector Lending', *Reserve Bank of India*, 2011, http://www.rbi.org.in/scripts/faqview.aspx?id=8

9   Ibid.

10   DFIs refer to Development Finance Institutions set up with the objective of driving development and focus largely

on emerging markets. One of the most well known DFIs is International Finance Corporation (IFC) setup by the World Bank. Several developed economies such as the USA, UK and several European countries have also set up funds with similar objectives. All these institutions together are labelled Development Finance Institutions.

11 'Master Circular- Introduction of New Category of NBFCs - 'Non Banking Financial Company-Micro Finance Institutions' (NBFC-MFIs) - Direction', *Reserve Bank of India*, https://www.rbi.org.in/commonperson/English/Scripts/Notification.aspx?Id=1022

12 Source: Micrometer, Issue 49 (Data as on 31 Mar 2024)

13 Private equity fund returns are usually benchmarked by vintage. All the funds launched in the same year are considered while benchmarking returns.

2. Trillions Are Needed

1 'Milton Friedman was an American economist and statistician who was awarded the Nobel Prize in Economic Sciences in 1976.' *Nobel Prize*, https://www.nobelprize.org/prizes/economic-sciences/1976/friedman/biographical/4o

2 'Milton Friedman - I, Pencil', *YouTube*, https://www.youtube.com/watch?v=67tHtpac5ws

3 Ibid.

4 Chapter 2, *How to Avoid a Climate Disaster – The Solutions We Have and the Breakthroughs We Need* by Bill Gates

5 'The cost of achieving the Sustainable Development Goals', *UNCTAD*, 2023, https://unctad.org/sdg-costing/about#:~:text=The%20resulting%20cost%20estimates%20for,annually%20from%202023%20to%202030

3. And Trillions Can Be Made

1 'Better Business, Better World', *United Nations Global Compact*, 2017, https://d306pr3pise04h.cloudfront.net/docs/news_events%2F9.3%2Fbetter-business-better-world.pdf

2 Sam Farber, *Wikipedia*, 2024, https://en.wikipedia.org/wiki/Sam_Farber#:~:text=Farber%20founded%20OXO%20as%20a,peeler%20with%20a%20standard%20design

3 'The untold story of the vegetable peeler that changed the world', *Fast Company*, 2018, https://www.fastcompany.com/90239156/the-untold-story-of-the-vegetable-peeler-that-changed-the-world

4 'The heartwarming story behind Nike's first hands-free shoe', *NDTV*, 2021, https://www.ndtv.com/offbeat/the-heartwarming-story-behind-nikes-first-hands-free-shoe-2361922

4. Early Trends Are Positive

1 'Morgan Stanley Institute for Sustainable Investing: Sustainable Reality FY2023', *Morgan Stanley*, 2023, https://www.morganstanley.com/content/dam/msdotcom/en/assets/pdfs/MSInstituteforSustainableInvesting-SustainableRealityFY2023-Final.pdf

2 '2023 GIINSIGHT Impact Investor Demographics – Figure 4', *GIIN*, 2023, https://s3.amazonaws.com/giin-web-assets/giin/assets/publication/research/2023-giinsight-impact-investor-demographics.pdf

3 'GIIN Annual Impact Investor Survey 2020: Executive Summary', *GIIN*, 2020, https://s3.amazonaws.com/giin-

web-assets/giin/assets/publication/research/giin-annual-impact-investor-survey-2020-executive-summary.pdf

4   '2022-12 Sustainable & Impact Investing Survey', *Cambridge Associates*, 2022, https://www.cambridgeassociates.com

5. What Is Impact Investing?

1   'Maya Chorengel on building the impact investing industry', *McKinsey & Company*, 2023, https://www.mckinsey.com/industries/private-capital/our-insights/maya-chorengel-on-building-the-impact-investing-industry.

2   Elon Musk, *X (formerly Twitter)*, 2022, https://x.com/elonmusk/status/1526957672200908801

3   Elon Musk, *X (formerly Twitter)*, 2022, https://x.com/elonmusk/status/1526958110023245829

4   'Is Elon Musk confused about ESG, or does Tesla have a point about impact?', *Socialsuite*, 2022, https://www.socialsuitehq.com/articles/is-elon-musk-confused-about-esg-or-does-tesla-have-a-point-about-impact

5   'This is Why Tesla's ESG Rating Isn't Great', *Morningstar*, 2023, https://www.morningstar.co.uk/uk/news/221629/this-is-why-teslas-esg-rating-isnt-great.aspx

6   Chapter 7, *How to Avoid a Climate Disaster: The Solutions We Have and the Breakthroughs We Need*, Bill Gates, 2021.

7   Elon Musk confused about ESG, or does Tesla have a point about impact', *Socialsuite* https://www.socialsuitehq.com/articles/is-elon-musk-confused-about-esg-or-does-tesla-have-a-point-about-impact

8   'What is ESG investing? MSCI ratings focus on corporate bottom line', *Bloomberg*, https://www.bloomberg.com/graphics/2021-what-is-esg-investing-msci-ratings-focus-on-corporate-bottom-line/

9   'Demand for beef means demand for more cows, which emit methane, which causes twenty-eight times more warming per molecule than carbon dioxide, in their excretions.' Source: *How to Avoid a Climate Disaster* by Bill Gates

10   'Moody's to refine ESG methodology', *Environment Analyst*, https://environment-analyst.com/global/107880/moodys-to-refine-esg-methodology

11   'Scrapping ESG credit indicators doesn't change the ESG rating narrative', *Euromoney*, https://www.euromoney.com/article/2c2eb8tqpr6gr1ggnuy9s/esg/scrapping-esg-credit-indicators-doesnt-change-the-esg-rating-narrative

12   'Impact investing: An introduction', *Rockefeller Philanthropy Advisors*, https://www.rockpa.org/guide/impact-investing-introduction/

13   'Investing for Impact - The Global Impact Investing Market 2020', *IFC*

14   'The Sustainable Development Goals (SDGs)', *United Nations*, [date], https://sdgs.un.org/goals

15   GIINSIGHT – Impact Measurement & Management Practice – Figure 4 https://s3.amazonaws.com/giin-web-assets/giin/assets/publication/research/2023-giinsight-%E2%80%93-impact-measurement-and-management-practice.pdf

16   '9 Principles', *Impact Principles*, https://www.impactprinciples.org/9-principles.

17   'Facts and Figures', *DWS*, https://www.dws.com/en-sg/our-profile/facts-and-figures/

18   'DWS and the Global Crackdown on Greenwashing', *Morningstar*, https://www.morningstar.co.uk/uk/news/226564/dws-and-the-global-crackdown-on-greenwashing.aspx.

Part 2: The Secrets of H.I.T. Investors

6. AC Ventures: Empowering MSMEs in Indonesia Through e-Commerce and Financial Services

1   Joseph Fewsmith, 'China in 1998: Tacking to Stay the Course', *Asian Survey*, 1999, Vol. 39, No. 1, pp. 99–113, http://www.jstor.com/stable/2645599

2   'Final Report of the 1998 Floods in the People's Republic of China', *United Nations Disaster Assessment and Coordination Team (UNDAC)*, 7–25 September 1998, https://reliefweb. int/report/china/final-report-1998-floods-peoples-republic-china#disaster

3   Multiple on invested capital

4   As of Q4 2022

5   Multiple on invested capital

6   'Scaling Impact with Technology', *BCG*, published in partnership with AC Ventures

7   Ibid.

8   In a USD 250 million fund, nearly USD 40 million gets set aside for fees and expenses.

9   Joseph Men, 'Andreessen Expands Venture Capital Business', *Financial Times*, 3 November 2010, https://www.ft.com/content/af5c1a7c-e717-11df-880d-00144feab49a?ftcamp=rss#axzz1gRgXwx3C

10 Investors in funds are usually called Limited Partners or LPs.

11 Net Promoter Score (NPS) is a widely used metric to measure customer satisfaction. It is measured by asking customers the likelihood that they would recommend a company. The percentage of customers who are unlikely to recommend (detractors) is subtracted from the percentage of customers who are likely to recommend (promoters) to arrive at NPS.

12 'World's Largest Economies 2050: Indonesia Projected in Top 5', *Invest Indonesia*, 2025, https://investindonesia. co.id/2025/01/07/worlds-largest-economies-2050-indonesia-projected-in-top-5/

7. Apis Partners: Building a Cashless Way to Inclusion

1   Donaldson, Lufkin & Jenrette (DLJ) was a U.S. investment bank founded by William H. Donaldson, Richard Jenrette, and Dan Lufkin in 1959. It was acquired by Credit Suisse in August 2000, for USD 11.5 billion.
2   'The Countries That Would Profit Most from a Cashless World', *Harvard Business Review*, May 2016, https://hbr. org/2016/05/the-countries-that-would-profit-most-from-a-cashless-world
3   'How Cashless Payments Help Economies Grow', *BCG*, 2019, https://www.bcg.com/publications/2019/cashless-payments-help-economies-grow
4   'Covid-19 Drives Global Surge in use of Digital Payments', *World Bank*, 29 June 2022, https://www.worldbank.org/en/news/press-release/2022/06/29/covid-19-drives-global-surge-in-use-of-digital-payments
5   'Returns with Responsibility DPO Group's Impact Journey: 2nd November 2021', *https://www.youtube.com/watch?v=NuxmYpYk_4g*
6   Organic growth refers to the growth achieved by the business without accounting for acquisitions.
7   CDC (Commonwealth Development Corporation) has been renamed as British International Investment (BII).

8. Capria Ventures: Solving Critical Challenges Across the Global South

1　Dave Richards, 'CEO Wisdom Podcast', *YouTube*, December 2023, https://www.youtube.com/watch?v=if_G-mplY9g&t=65s

2　Today, World Vision's micro-finance subsidiaries operate in thirty countries worldwide.

3　Muhammad Yunus is a Bangladeshi social entrepreneur, banker, economist and civil society leader who was awarded the Nobel Peace Prize in 2006 for founding the Grameen Bank and pioneering the concepts of microcredit and microfinance, which are loans given to entrepreneurs too poor to qualify for traditional bank loans.

4　Avocado is considered an expensive luxury fruit only consumed by the more well off in emerging markets. Avocado start-ups is the nickname used for businesses that serve this narrow segment.

5　Please refer https://capria.vc/impact-reports/ for all the impact reports.

6　BoP comprises the 1.05 billion people in India (5 out of 6 Indians) who live on an annual household income of less than Rs 2,00,000 (USD 3,200) as of 2005. According to a 2007 McKinsey analysis, by 2015, size of the BoP is projected to be 997 million, nearly 80 per cent of the population.

7　Unit economics refers to contribution profit per unit which is calculated as per unit revenue minus per unit variable cost.

8　Multiple On Invested Capital

9. Future Planet Capital: Scaling Innovation for People and Planet

1   Carol J. Loomis, 'Warren Buffet's Wild Ride at Salomon', *Forbes Magazine,* 27 October 1997. https://fortune.com/article/warren-buffett-salomon/ Also see, Charles R. Geisst, *The Last Partnerships: Inside the Great Wall Street Dynasties,* McGraw-Hill (2001)
2   Interview with author, 2024.
3   An enhanced index fund seeks to enhance the returns of an index by using active management to modify the weights of holdings for additional return.
4   'What Are the Principles for Responsible Investment', *UN PRI,* https://www.unpri.org/about-us/what-are-the-principles-for-responsible-investment
5   'What Is Responsible Investment', *UN PRI,* https://www.unpri.org/introductory-guides-to-responsible-investment/what-is-responsible-investment/4780.article
6   Interview with author, 2024.
7   'Sustainable Investing Journey', *Robeco,* https://www.robeco.com/en-me/sustainable-investing/journey
8   Iain Harris, 'Pokemon Go Captures $2bn in Player Spending', *PocketGamer,* 26 September 2018, https://www.pocketgamer.biz/pokemon-go-captures-over-2bn-through-player-spending/
9   Joris Beerda, 'The Real Reason Pokemon Go is Failing', *The Octalysis Group,* https://octalysisgroup.com/2017/09/why-pokemon-go-is-failing/ Also see, Mark Humphrey-Jenner, 'From Favourite to Failing: What Went Wrong with Pokemon Go?', *Sydney Morning Herald,* 15 October 2016, https://www.smh.com.au/opinion/from-favourite-to-failing-what-went-wrong-with-pokemon-go-20161019-gs5pbb.html

10 Quantis, 2018
11 Rissanen, 2020
12 International Monetary Fund, 2022
13 European Parliament, 29 December 2020
14 Bloomberg, 20 August 2019
15 Statista/O'Neill, 1 December 2023
16 Rissanen, 2020
17 The name 401(k) is after the subsection 401(k) of the United States Internal Revenue Code in which the plan is defined.

10. Lok Capital: Driving Financial Inclusion in India

1 'The Fortune at the Bottom of the Pyramid', *Financial Express*, 21 May 2018, https://www.financialexpress.com/opinion/the-fortune-at-the-bottom-of-pyramid/1174864/
2 C.K. Prahalad, *Fortune at the Bottom of the Pyramid*, pp 3–10.
3 Ibid.
4 Neelima Mahajan Bansal, 'CK Prahalad: The Inclusive Visionary', *Forbes Magazine*, 3 May 2010, https://www.forbesindia.com/article/special/ck-prahalad-the-inclusive-visionary/12892/1
5 Aravind, with its mission to 'eliminate needless blindness', provides large volume, high quality and affordable care. 50 per cent of its patients receive services either free of cost or at steeply subsidised rate, yet the organization remains financially self-sustainable. Much importance is given to equity—ensuring that all patients are accorded the same high-quality care and service, regardless of their economic status. A critical component of Aravind's model is the high patient volume, which brings with it the benefits of economies of scale. Aravind Eye Care started off as

an eleven-bed hospital in 1976. Today, Aravind operates a growing network of eye care facilities, a postgraduate institute, a management training and consulting institute, an ophthalmic manufacturing unit, a research institute and eye banks. Aravind's eye care facilities include fourteen eye hospitals, six outpatient eye examination centres and 108 primary eye care facilities in South India. Source: https://aravind.org/our-story/

6   Warburg is one of the largest private equity firms globally and has invested more than USD 120 billion in more than 1,000 companies across 40+ countries. https://warburgpincus.com/firm/

7   Before joining the firm in 2017, Vijay was co-president of Franklin Templeton Investments, where in a career of more than twenty years, he was responsible for long-term strategic initiatives and the firm's investment management, trading and global retail and institutional channels. Prior to joining Franklin Templeton, Vijay spent eleven years at the World Bank advising governments on developing their financial markets and arranging equity, quasi-equity and debt financing.

8   Carried Interest refers to the share of profits received by the Fund Manager for generating good performance. In Private Equity, fund managers usually receive 20 per cent of the profits over an above a certain threshold (called hurdle) around 6-8 per cent.

9   Internal Rate of Return signifies the average return per annum.

10   IRIS is an impact measurement framework developed by Global Impact Investing Network (GIIN).

11. Quona Capital: The Fintech Revolution

1 Quona Capital, 'A Youth Spent in El Salvador and Spain Brings Quona's Jonathan Whittle to Investments in Latin America', *Medium.com*, 4 September 2019, https://quona-capital.medium.com/a-youth-spent-in-el-salvador-and-spain-brings-quonas-jonathan-whittle-to-investments-in-latin-

2 Ibid.

3 Interview with author.

4 POS device stands for point-of-sale device. It is the machine that credit cards and debit cards are swiped on.

5 Interview with author.

6 Ibid.

7 https://tracxn.com/d/unicorns/unicorns-in-brazil/__8h yB0gzx2OtUvKmJSyeRmYi5_7jls2YD01MABluXkeQ #t-9-creditas

8 'Grain Commerce Platform Arya.ag Raises $60 Mn from Asia Impact SA, Others', *VCCircle*, 2025, https://www.vccircle.com/grain-commerce-platform-arya-ag-raises-60-mn-from-asia-impact-sa-others.

9 'Agritech Start-up Arya.ag Raises $29 Million from Blue Earth Capital', *The Economic Times*, 2024, https://economictimes.indiatimes.com/tech/funding/agritech-start-up-aryaag-raises-29-million-from-blue-earth-capital/articleshow/111636934.cms?from=mdr

10 Interview with author.

11 Interview with author.

12 Ibid.

12. Sustainable Development Capital LLP: Energy Efficiency Is Core to Achieving Net Zero

1   BAU—Business as usual
2   Maxwell, Jonathan, *The EDGE: How competition for resources is pushing the world, and its climate, to the brink*, Harriman House, Great Britain, 2023.

13. Verdane: Decarbonization and Digitalization with Sustainability at the Core

1   'HEC Paris-Dow Jones 2023 Growth Capital & Performance Ranking Results Challenge Conventional Wisdom: Large Funds Underperform', *HEC Paris Newsroom*, 2023, https://www.hec.edu/en/news-room/ hec-paris-dow-jones-2023-growth-capital-performance- ranking-results-challenge-conventional-wisdom-large- funds-underperform
2   Related to ancient or medieval Norway or Scandinavia
3   Verdandi, Urd and Skuld form the trio of goddesses deciding the fate of people.
4   Buyout funds usually take controlling stakes in the companies while growth funds primarily focus on minority stakes and providing capital to support growth.
5   'About', *NORNORM*, https://nornorm.com/about.
6   Scope 1 emissions include emissions from sources directly controlled by the company. Scope 2 includes emissions caused by the company indirectly from the energy purchased by it. Scope 3 includes emissions across the value chain of a company that it is indirectly responsible for.

Scan QR code to access the
Penguin Random House India website